Sunset

Poultry
COOK BOOK

*By the Editors of
Sunset Books and Sunset Magazine*

Sunset Publishing Corporation ▪ **Menlo Park, California**

Clusters of tiny, deep purple "champagne grapes" enhance chicken legs in a simple wine sauce. The recipe for Sautéed Chicken with Corinth Grapes is on page 69.

Research & Text
SUE BROWNLEE

Contributing Editor
REBECCA LABRUM

Coordinating Editor
DEBORAH THOMAS KRAMER

Design
SANDRA POPOVICH

Illustrations
SANDRA BRUCE

Photographers
KEVIN SANCHEZ: 47, 50, 55, 99.
DARROW M. WATT: 2. **TOM WYATT:** 10, 15, 18, 23, 26, 31, 39, 42, 58, 63, 66, 71, 74, 79, 82, 87, 90, 95, 102, 110, 115, 118. **NIKOLAY ZUREK:** 7, 34, 107, 123, 126.

Photo Stylist
SUSAN MASSEY-WEIL

COVER: Tomatoes with a sprinkling of olive oil and cracked black pepper complement Chicken with Olives & Pine Nuts (recipe on page 70). Design by Susan Bryant. Photography by Tom Wyatt. Photo styling by Susan Massey-Weil. Food styling by Sue Brownlee.

ABOUT THE RECIPES

All of the recipes in this book were tested and developed in the *Sunset* test kitchens.

Food and Entertaining Editor, *Sunset* Magazine
JERRY ANNE DI VECCHIO

Editor, Sunset Books: Elizabeth L. Hogan

First printing May 1991

■ POULTRY POINTS

Counting the benefits of poultry? They make a long list. Poultry scores high with both cooks and diners.

Chicken and turkey pieces, widely available in today's markets, have become favorite choices. Boned and skinned parts or ground meat are quick and easy to prepare. Poultry pieces are economical, and they let you match purchases to dining preferences.

Our recipes take advantage of today's tastes. Chapters cover whole birds, cut-up parts, ground, and even cooked poultry. Other fowl, including game hen, quail, and duck, are discussed. Poultry's versatility is showcased in a variety of techniques—from baking to barbecuing—and cuisines ranging from Southeast Asian to Southwestern.

We feature options for health-conscious cooks, capitalizing on poultry's high protein and low fat—though special splurges are also included. Recipes for appetizers, soups, snacks, salads, sandwiches, and main courses will please poultry fans at both simple and formal meals.

We wish to thank Dr. George K. York and Dr. Gideon Zeidler, Food Technologists, and John C. Voris, Area Turkey Specialist at the University of California's Cooperative Extension for offering their time and advice.

We extend our sincere appreciation to Karen Ross for her assistance with food styling—and to Cottonwood, Fillamento, RH, and Best of All Worlds for props used in our photographs. We offer special thanks to Dave Schaub and his staff at Schaub's Meat, Fish & Poultry; to Ken Fujimoto at Monterey Market; to Beltramo's Wine & Spirits; and to Whole Foods Market.

With our recipes, we provide nutritional analyses (see page 9) prepared by Hill Nutrition Associates, Inc., of Florida. We are grateful to Lynne Hill, R.D., for her expert advice.

Contents

SPECIAL FEATURES

Serving Up Poultry

WHOLE & HALVES & QUARTERS &

BREASTS & LEGS & THIGHS & WINGS &

DRUMMETTES & GROUND &

Chicken and turkey were once reserved for Sunday suppers and holiday feasts. Today, though, both birds come to the table any day of the week, any time of year—and not just as whole poultry. The chicken and turkey pieces so widely available in modern markets have made poultry a favorite for everyday meals.

APPEALING ASSETS

Why are poultry parts so popular among today's busy cooks? First of all, chicken and turkey pieces allow quick and easy preparation; boned, skinned pieces and ground poultry in particular get meals off to a fast start.

Convenience isn't the only asset poultry offers—it's an economical choice, as well. Of course, price varies with the pieces you choose: cost per pound is less for whole birds, higher for boneless, skinless breast meat. The best buy for you depends in part on your dining habits. If you prefer light meat, you'll cut down on waste, and thus ultimately spend less, by purchasing only breasts. Likewise, keep in mind the yield per pound for various parts. According to USDA figures, a whole chicken is 53% edible meat; breasts are 63% edible, thighs 60%, drumsticks 53%, wings 30%, and back and neck 27%.

Poultry's popularity can also be traced to the health benefits it offers. It's a good source of protein and is generally lower in calories than most red meats, particularly if you opt for skinless white meat. Skinned chicken and turkey breast also contain less saturated fat than most red meats, a strong selling point for diners watching their cholesterol. The nutritional values of several poultry types are summarized in the chart below.

NUTRITIONAL VALUES OF POULTRY

Portion: 3 ounces cooked	Calories	Protein (g)	Total fat (g)	Saturated fat (g)	Cholesterol (mg)
CHICKEN					
Breast, meat and skin, roasted	168	25	7	2	71
Breast, meat only, roasted	140	26	3	1	72
Thigh, meat and skin, roasted	210	21	13	4	79
Thigh, meat only, roasted	178	22	9	3	81
Drumstick, meat and skin, roasted	184	23	9	3	77
Drumstick, meat only, roasted	146	24	5	1	79
Liver, simmered	134	21	5	2	537
TURKEY					
Breast, meat and skin, roasted	161	24	6	2	63
Breast, meat only, roasted	131	25	2	1	59
Leg, meat and skin, roasted	177	24	8	3	72
Leg, meat only, roasted	157	24	6	2	75
Giblets (gizzard, heart, liver), simmered	142	23	4	1	356
Ground, regular, cooked	195	21	12	3	59
GOOSE					
Meat and skin, roasted	259	21	19	6	77
Meat only, roasted	202	25	11	4	82
DUCK					
Meat and skin, roasted	287	16	24	8	71
Meat only, roasted	171	20	10	4	76

Finally, poultry is wonderfully versatile. Serve it as an appetizer, in a salad, soup, or sandwich, as a main course or a snack, hot or cold. Choose it for your fanciest party or homiest supper; present it simply or with an elaborate sauce. Cook it any way you like: baked, braised, broiled, barbecued, sautéed, steeped, steamed, smoked, stir-fried. Season it with hot chiles or sweet spices, with citrus juices, wine, soy sauce, or mustard. For any cook, poultry offers almost limitless possibilities.

POULTRY TYPES

Almost all markets offer both fresh chicken and turkey; some stores also feature a selection of other poultry, such as game hens and quail.

BROILERS. Also called frying chickens and broiler-fryers, broilers account for about 90% of all the chicken marketed in the United States. And for good reason, too—they're the perfect all-purpose birds, suitable for roasting, simmering, and grilling as well as for broiling and frying. Broilers are usually about 7 weeks old and typically weigh 3 to 3½ pounds, although weights may range from 2½ to 5 pounds. You can purchase these chickens whole, cut up, and as individual parts.

ROASTERS. In general, all chickens weighing 5 pounds or more are classed as roasters. The average roaster weight is 5 to 6 pounds, though some birds may be as heavy as 8 pounds. Usually about 2½ months old, these chickens provide more servings than broilers do; they're a good choice if you're planning a roast chicken dinner for a big party.

CAPONS. A capon is a surgically desexed male chicken. Meaty and tender, capons are excellent for roasting. They're usually about 4 months old and weigh about 9½ pounds.

HEAVY HENS. Weighing in at 4½ to 6 pounds, these chickens aren't much heavier than broilers or roasters; they are, however, a good deal older (about 15 months), less tender, and less available in markets. Heavy hens are also called stewing hens—and as that name implies, they're best in slowly simmered dishes such as stews and soups.

TURKEYS. Whole turkeys range in weight from 8 to 36 pounds. Generally, birds under 16 pounds are hens, while those over 16 pounds are toms. Hens and toms don't differ in flavor or texture, but heavier birds typically do have a higher proportion of meat to bone. Almost all commercially sold turkeys are labeled "young" turkeys; they're usually 4 to 6 months old.

Birds under 4 months old are sold as fryer-roaster turkeys. Age does affect quality: the younger the turkey, the milder and more tender the meat.

OTHER BIRDS. Cornish game hens, ducks, geese, pheasants, quail, and squab are discussed in special features throughout this book.

POULTRY PIECES

Both chicken and turkey are sold as individual parts and as ground meat.

BREASTS. You'll find *chicken breast halves* sold in several ways: boneless and skinless (about 4 oz. per breast half); skinned, but with the bone in (6 to 6½ oz. per breast half, yielding 4 oz. meat); and complete with bones and skin (about 8 oz. per breast half, yielding 4 oz. meat). Many of the recipes in this book use skinless, boneless breast halves, also called fillets and typically sold four to a package.

Boned turkey breast half (or roast) is sold with or without the skin. *Bone-in turkey breast* is also available, usually with the skin on; it yields about a pound of meat for every 1¼ to 1⅓ pounds weight (with skin).

Turkey breast slices (or cutlets) are thin (⅛- to ⅜-inch) crosswise slices cut from boned, skinned breast.

Turkey tenderloin (or fillet) is a boneless whole muscle from the inside center of a breast half. Large tenderloins, weighing about 8 ounces, are usually sold two to a package; smaller ones come three or four to a package. When split lengthwise, tenderloins may be labeled "tenderloin steaks."

Chicken or turkey breast strips (sometimes called stir-fry strips, tenders, or chicken tenderloins) are boneless pieces ready to use for stir-frying.

THIGHS & LEGS. *Chicken thighs* are available boned and skinned, usually in 1-pound packages; they're also sold with bones and skin. To get a pound of meat, you'll need to buy 1¾ to 2 pounds bone-in, skin-on thighs.

Turkey thigh is sold boned (usually two thighs to a package) and bone-in. One medium-size bone-in thigh (about 1½ lbs.) yields 1 pound meat.

Whole chicken legs (thighs with drumsticks attached) are usually sold two to a package; they weigh about 8 ounces each.

Chicken drumsticks typically come six to a package; each piece weighs about 4 ounces. *Turkey drumsticks* weigh 1 to 1¼ pounds each and are generally sold three to a package.

WINGS. You'll usually find *chicken wings* 10 to 12 to a 2-pound package; *drummettes*, the meatiest part of the

For a festive autumn supper, offer Grilled Quail with Pasta (recipe on page 104). The juicy butterflied birds, hot from the grill, are served atop wide pasta ribbons tossed with fresh Roma tomatoes, mushrooms, and smoky pancetta.

wing, come about 15 to a 1¼-pound package. *Turkey wings* generally weigh about 12 ounces each and are sold two to a package.

GROUND POULTRY. Both *ground chicken* and *ground turkey* consist primarily of dark meat. Ground turkey resembles ground beef in flavor and texture, while ground chicken has a milder flavor and a pastier, moister texture. For ground poultry that's lower in fat and calories, buy ground skinned breast meat (you may need to have your meat market grind it for you).

PURCHASING POULTRY

Make sure any fresh poultry you buy has been kept refrigerated. When purchasing prepackaged poultry, select trays with little or no liquid in the bottom. If the packaged poultry you choose is frozen, avoid torn packages and those containing frozen liquid; both these conditions may be signs of moisture loss or of partial thawing and refreezing, leading to a decrease in the quality of the meat.

When buying whole chicken and turkey, look for plump birds with smooth, tight skin. Turkeys should have cream-colored skin; a chicken's skin color may range from nearly white to deep yellow, depending on the bird's diet, its age, and the methods used in processing.

In general, buy about 1 pound of whole chicken per serving; allow 1 pound of whole turkey per serving (2 pounds if you want ample leftovers).

STORING POULTRY

Fresh poultry should be cooked within 2 days of purchase; if you can't use it within that time, freeze it (see the chart below for storage times).

To refrigerate poultry, leave it in the market's wrap to avoid introducing bacteria by repeated handling. (If the wrapping is torn, though, do replace it with wax paper, plastic wrap, or foil.) Place the poultry in the coldest part of the refrigerator. If you plan to stuff a whole bird, keep poultry and stuffing *separate* for refrigeration.

To freeze poultry, enclose it in heavy freezer paper, plastic wrap, or foil; to prevent freezer burn, be sure the wrap is airtight. Label and date all packages, and use older items first. Don't stuff whole birds before freezing them.

THAWING POULTRY

The safest way to thaw all poultry is simply to let it stand, well wrapped, in the refrigerator. Allow 12 to 16 hours for a whole chicken and 4 to 9 hours for chicken parts, depending on the size and number in package. For whole turkey, allow 1 to 2 days if the bird weighs 8 to 12 pounds; allow 2 to 3 days for a 12- to 16-pound bird, 3 to 4 days for a 16- to 20-pounder, and 4 to 5 days for a 20- to 24-pounder. Turkey parts take 1 to 2 days.

If you must thaw poultry quickly, enclose it in a watertight plastic bag, then place in cold water;

COLD STORAGE OF POULTRY

Product	Refrigerator (Days at 40°F)	Freezer (Months at 0°F)
FRESH POULTRY		
Chicken and turkey (whole)	1 to 2	12
Chicken and turkey pieces	1 to 2	9
Duck and goose (whole)	1 to 2	6
Giblets	1 to 2	3 to 4
COOKED POULTRY		
Covered with broth or gravy	1 to 2	6
Pieces not in broth or gravy	3 to 4	4
Cooked poultry dishes	3 to 4	4 to 6
Fried chicken	3 to 4	4

Source: A Quick Consumer Guide to Safe Food Handling, United States Department of Agriculture Food Safety and Inspection Service, September 1990

change the water frequently. You can also thaw poultry in your microwave oven according to the manufacturer's instructions. *Do not thaw poultry in warm water or at room temperature:* bacteria can develop rapidly under these conditions.

■ TESTING FOR DONENESS

The type of bird, the cut, and the cooking method will all influence the test you use to determine doneness. For chicken and turkey, one technique that works well in almost all cases is to cut the meat in the thickest part (or to the bone); it should no longer be pink in the center (or near the bone). *Note:* Birds such as goose and pheasant may require special tests; refer to our features for help.

For a whole chicken or turkey, a meat thermometer offers the most accurate doneness test. You can either insert a regular thermometer before roasting or check the temperature occasionally with an instant-read thermometer. Consult your thermometer well before the suggested total cooking time is up: because the rate of cooking varies with a bird's shape, even birds of identical weight may be done at different times. Check birds weighing less than 12 pounds at least 30 minutes before they should be done, larger birds at least 1 hour ahead. Then read the thermometer again about every 15 minutes until the desired temperature is reached.

To check breast temperature, insert the thermometer straight down through the thickest part of the breast until it touches the bone; or insert it horizontally, about halfway between the wing joint and the tip of the breastbone. A 160°F reading means the breast is done (the concurrent temperature in the center of the thickest part of the breast, *not* touching the bone, will be 170°F).

To check thigh meat, insert the thermometer into the thigh between body and leg, almost to the thigh joint; it should read 180° to 185°F. Usually, but not always, the breast is done before the thigh (the drumstick will be done in either case). In this instance, remove the bird from the oven when the breast is done; carve the breast, then continue to cook the thighs, skin side down, in a shallow pan in a 450° oven until the meat near the bone is no longer pink (about 10 more minutes).

■ SAFETY GUIDELINES

All poultry is a potential host for the organisms that cause spoilage and food poisoning. To avoid problems, be sure you follow proper storage, cooking, and handling procedures. Remember that the bacteria, yeasts, and molds that cause food to spoil grow more rapidly at higher temperatures; for this reason, it's wise—especially if the weather is hot—to make poultry the last item on your shopping list, and then get it home and into the refrigerator quickly. If your trip home is a long one, consider taking along a cooler with frozen ice packs to hold your purchases. Be aware that spoilage organisms continue to grow even in food refrigerated at 40°F or lower; luckily, though, most such "bugs" make themselves known. If poultry has an off odor or looks bad, throw it out.

Unfortunately, the bacteria that cause food poisoning don't announce their presence so clearly: most of them can't be seen, smelled, or tasted. The best way to protect yourself against these organisms is to keep cold foods cold and hot foods hot. At low refrigerator temperatures (40°F or lower), most food poisoning bacteria don't grow; at the high temperatures (160° to 212°F) reached in roasting, baking, boiling, and frying, they're killed. Typical holding temperatures for cooked food (at least 140°F) keep bacteria from growing, but don't kill them; and when cooked food is left to stand, the possibility for bacterial growth rises rapidly as the food drops to room temperature. Be sure you keep poultry cold until cooking. Refrigerate leftovers as quickly as possible, always storing stuffing separately; and in any case, never let cooked food stand at room temperature for more than 2 hours.

Finally, take steps to prevent the spread of bacteria. After working with raw poultry, thoroughly wash your hands, tools, and work surfaces with hot, soapy water. To sanitize work surfaces and tools, treat them with diluted chlorine bleach (2 to 3 teaspoons of bleach per quart of water) and rinse well.

ABOUT OUR NUTRITIONAL DATA

For our recipes, we provide a nutritional analysis stating calorie count; grams of protein, carbohydrates, total fat, and saturated fat; and milligrams of cholesterol and sodium. Generally, the analysis applies to a single serving, based on the number of servings given for each recipe and the amount of each ingredient. If a range is given for the number of servings and/or the amount of an ingredient, the analysis is based on an average of the figures given.

The nutritional analysis does not include optional ingredients or those for which no specific amount is stated. If an ingredient is listed with a substitution, the information was calculated using the first choice.

A golden, creamy purée of carrot, onion, and pan juices makes a simple
sauce for rosemary-fragrant Roast Chicken & Potatoes (recipe on page 12).
Fresh Brussels sprouts are a bright and tasty accompaniment for the
crisp-crusted potatoes, sweet garlic cloves, and tender meat.

Plump Birds & Cut-up Pieces

ROASTED & BRAISED & BARBECUED &

STUFFED & HERBED & SAUCED & GLAZED &

DRESSED & BASTED & NOODLED & CASSEROLED &

ROAST CHICKEN & POTATOES

Preparation time: About 15 minutes

Roasting time: 1 to 1¼ hours

No matter how crisp and delicious the bird, a bowl of lumpy gravy can put a damper on a roast chicken dinner. But no need to worry here: just cook carrots and onions with the chicken, then blend the vegetables and pan juices to make a foolproof, flavorful sauce.

> 1¼ **pounds small thin-skinned potatoes (***each*** 1½ to 2 inches in diameter), scrubbed and cut in half**
>
> 1 **small onion, cut in half**
>
> 1 **small carrot, quartered**
>
> ½ **cup garlic cloves, peeled**
>
> 1 **teaspoon minced fresh rosemary or ½ teaspoon dry rosemary**
>
> ¼ **cup butter or margarine, cut into small chunks**
>
> 1 **chicken (4 to 4½ lbs.)**
>
> ¾ **to 1 cup regular-strength chicken broth**
> **Salt and pepper**

Place potatoes (cut side down), onion, carrot, and garlic cloves in a 9- by 13-inch baking pan. Sprinkle with rosemary and dot with butter.

Reserve chicken neck and giblets for other uses; pull off and discard lumps of fat from chicken. Rinse chicken inside and out, pat dry, and place, breast up, atop vegetables. Roast, uncovered, in a 400° oven for 30 minutes; brush chicken with pan juices. Return to oven. Continue to roast, basting often, until meat near thighbone is no longer pink; cut to test (30 to 45 more minutes).

Tilt chicken to drain juices from cavity into pan. Transfer chicken, potatoes, and half the garlic to a platter; keep warm.

Scrape onion, carrot, remaining garlic, and pan juices into a food processor or blender; whirl until smoothly puréed, adding enough broth to make a pourable sauce. Pour sauce into a small serving bowl. Serve chicken and vegetables with sauce; add salt and pepper to taste. Makes 4 servings.

Per serving: 967 calories, 66 g protein, 34 g carbohydrates, 62 g fat, 21 g saturated fat, 277 mg cholesterol, 583 mg sodium

ROAST CHICKEN WITH BEETS, SQUASH & ONIONS

Preparation time: About 15 minutes

Roasting time: 1 to 1¼ hours

Small whole onions plus a pair of unexpected vegetables—beets and banana squash—roast alongside an herb-seasoned whole chicken in this one-pan supper.

> 4 **small beets (***each*** about 1½ inches in diameter), tops removed, scrubbed (leave root ends intact)**
>
> 8 **small onions (***each*** about 1 inch in diameter), unpeeled**
>
> ¼ **cup olive oil**
>
> 2 **teaspoons *each* fresh thyme and rosemary leaves (or 1 teaspoon *each* dry leaves)**
>
> 1 **chicken (3½ to 4 lbs.)**
>
> 12 **ounces banana or Hubbard squash, peeled and cut into 2-inch chunks**
>
> **Thyme or rosemary sprigs**

Place beets and onions in opposite corners of a shallow 12- by 15-inch roasting pan. In a bowl, mix oil, thyme leaves, and rosemary leaves; brush some of the mixture over vegetables. Bake in a 375° oven for 10 minutes.

Increase oven temperature to 400°. Reserve chicken neck and giblets for other uses; pull off and discard lumps of fat from chicken. Rinse chicken inside and out, pat dry, and place, breast up, in center of pan. Place squash in an empty corner of pan. Brush chicken and vegetables with remaining oil mixture. Roast, uncovered, basting often with pan juices, until beets are tender when pierced and until meat near chicken thighbone is no longer pink; cut to test (45 minutes to 1 hour). Lift vegetables from pan with a slotted spoon; set aside. Tilt chicken to drain juices from cavity into pan; discard juices.

To serve, trim root ends from beets. Transfer chicken and vegetables to a platter and garnish with thyme sprigs. Makes 4 servings.

Per serving: 734 calories, 56 g protein, 17 g carbohydrates, 49 g fat, 12 g saturated fat, 192 mg cholesterol, 228 mg sodium

COUSCOUS WITH ROAST CHICKEN & VEGETABLES

Preparation time: About 20 minutes

Roasting time: 1 to 1¼ hours

When you roast a chicken, you get both a crisp golden bird and a bonus of savory pan juices. Here, we combine the juices with broth, couscous, and a variety of vegetables to create an appetizing, colorful supper.

　1　**chicken (3½ to 4 lbs.)**
　　　Pepper
　1　**small head fennel (about 1 lb.), base trimmed and coarse stalks cut off (reserve green leaves)**
　2　**tablespoons olive oil**
　1　**small head garlic**
　4　**medium-size zucchini (about 1½ lbs.** *total***), cut into 1-inch-thick slices**
　2　**large carrots (about 12 oz.** *total***), cut into 1-inch-thick slices**
　1　**large red bell pepper (about 6 oz.), seeded and cut into chunks**
　1　**large red onion, cut into eighths**
　3　**cups regular-strength chicken broth**
　2　**cups couscous**
　　　Salt

Reserve chicken neck and giblets for other uses; pull off and discard lumps of fat from chicken. Rinse chicken inside and out, pat dry, and place, breast up, on a rack in a 9- by 13-inch baking pan. Sprinkle liberally with pepper.

Rinse fennel and cut into 1-inch chunks.

Pour oil into a 10- by 15-inch baking pan. Place fennel, whole garlic, zucchini, carrots, bell pepper, and onion in pan; turn to coat with oil.

Roast chicken and vegetables, uncovered, in a 400° oven for 1 to 1¼ hours, switching pan positions halfway through roasting. Vegetables should be soft and beginning to blacken at edges; meat near thighbone should no longer be pink (cut to test).

Separate garlic into cloves; set aside. Coarsely chop vegetables; set aside. Tilt chicken to drain juices from cavity into pan. Transfer chicken to a platter; keep warm.

Skim and discard fat from pan juices. Add broth to pan and bring to a boil over high heat. Squeeze garlic cloves from skins into pan. Stir in couscous and vegetables. Cover, remove from heat, and let stand until liquid is absorbed (about 5 minutes). Spoon couscous around chicken; garnish with reserved fennel leaves and season to taste with salt. Makes 4 servings.

Per serving: 994 calories, 71 g protein, 98 g carbohydrates, 35 g fat, 8 g saturated fat, 165 mg cholesterol, 1,033 mg sodium

FIVE-SPICE ROAST CHICKEN

Preparation time: About 10 minutes

Roasting time: 1¼ to 1½ hours

Chinese spices quickly cooked together with soy and sherry season this flavorful roast chicken and the sauce that goes with it. Steamed broccoli and brown rice are good accompaniments for the meal.

　1　**teaspoon salad oil**
　1½　**teaspoons Chinese five-spice; or ½ teaspoon** *each* **anise seeds and ground ginger and ¼ teaspoon** *each* **ground cinnamon and ground cloves**
　3　**tablespoons soy sauce**
　1　**tablespoon** *each* **sugar and dry sherry**
　1　**clove garlic, minced**
　1　**large chicken (4½ to 5 lbs.)**
　3　**tablespoons minced green onions (including tops)**

In a small pan, stir oil with five-spice over medium heat until hot. Add soy, sugar, sherry, and garlic.

Reserve chicken neck and giblets for other uses; pull off and discard lumps of fat from chicken. Rinse chicken inside and out, pat dry, and place, breast up, on a rack in a 9- by 13-inch baking pan. Rub generously with five-spice mixture. Pour remaining mixture into chicken cavity.

Roast, uncovered, in a 400° oven until meat near thighbone is no longer pink; cut to test (1¼ to 1½ hours). Tilt chicken to drain juices from cavity into pan, then transfer bird to a platter. Stir pan juices to scrape up browned bits. Pour juices into a small pitcher, skim off fat, and add onions. Offer sauce with chicken. Makes 4 servings.

Per serving: 603 calories, 66 g protein, 6 g carbohydrates, 34 g fat, 9 g saturated fat, 209 mg cholesterol, 967 mg sodium

CHICKEN & NOODLES WITH PIMENTOS

Preparation time: About 20 minutes

Cooking time: About 1¼ hours

Bite-size pieces of roast chicken are tossed with pasta and slivered fresh pimentos in a piquant, orange-scented cream sauce. Garnish the dish with fresh cilantro leaves and crumbled crisp chicken skin (you can omit the skin, if you like).

- 1 **chicken (3½ to 4 lbs.)**
- 1 **large orange (about 8 oz.)**
- 2 **large fresh pimentos or red bell peppers (about 12 oz. *total*), seeded and cut into thin strips**
- 2 **cups whipping cream**
- 1 **teaspoon crushed dried hot red chiles**
  Salt and pepper
- 1 **package (9 or 10 oz.) fresh fettuccine or tagliarini**
- ½ **cup fresh cilantro (coriander) leaves**

Reserve chicken neck and giblets for other uses; pull off and discard lumps of fat from chicken. Rinse chicken inside and out, pat dry, and place, breast up, in a 9- by 13-inch baking pan. Roast, uncovered, in a 400° oven until meat near thighbone is no longer pink; cut to test (about 1 hour). Tilt chicken to drain juices from cavity into pan. Set chicken aside. Scrape juices, including browned bits, into a 10- to 12-inch frying pan; set aside.

When chicken is cool enough to handle, pull off skin in large pieces; place, fat side down, on a rack in baking pan. Return to 400° oven and roast, uncovered, until very crisp (about 15 minutes).

Meanwhile, remove and discard chicken bones; tear meat into bite-size pieces and set aside. With a zester, remove peel (colored part only) from orange. (Or use a vegetable peeler, then cut peel into fine strands with a knife.) Reserve orange for other uses.

Add pimentos to pan juices in frying pan; cook over medium-high heat, stirring often, until pimentos are slightly softened (about 3 minutes). Add cream, chiles, and half the orange peel. Increase heat to high and boil until reduced by half (about 5 minutes). Add chicken meat and cook just until hot; season to taste with salt and pepper.

Meanwhile, cook fettuccine according to package directions just until tender to bite. Drain well. Add pasta to chicken mixture; remove from heat and mix lightly, using 2 forks. Transfer to a deep platter. Crumble chicken skin over pasta; garnish with cilantro and remaining orange peel. Makes 6 servings.

Per serving: 570 calories, 37 g protein, 30 g carbohydrates, 33 g fat, 18 g saturated fat, 232 mg cholesterol, 129 mg sodium

Pictured on facing page

HOT & SWEET CHICKEN

Preparation time: About 10 minutes

Cooking time: About 55 minutes

A tangy, citrus-based sauce does double duty in this dish. You use part of it to coat a cut-up chicken during baking, then mix the rest with the pan juices to spoon over the cooked meat and hot, fluffy rice.

- 1 **tablespoon grated orange peel**
- 1 **cup orange juice**
- 3 **tablespoons lemon juice**
- 2 **tablespoons Worcestershire**
- 1 **tablespoon Dijon mustard**
- ½ **teaspoon liquid hot pepper seasoning**
- ½ **cup red currant jelly**
- 1 **chicken (3 to 3½ lbs.), cut up**
- 3 **cups hot cooked rice**
- 1 **tablespoon cornstarch mixed with 2 tablespoons water**

In a 1- to 1½-quart pan, combine orange peel, orange juice, lemon juice, Worcestershire, mustard, hot pepper seasoning, and jelly. Stir over medium heat until jelly is melted.

Rinse chicken and pat dry. Then arrange chicken, except breast pieces, skin side up in a shallow 12- by 15-inch roasting pan; brush with some of the orange sauce. Bake, uncovered, in a 400° oven for 20 minutes, basting with sauce after 10 minutes. Add breast pieces. Continue to bake, basting often, until meat near thighbone is no longer pink; cut to test (about 25 more minutes).

Arrange chicken and rice on a platter; keep warm. Skim and discard fat from pan juices; then add remaining orange sauce to pan. Add cornstarch mixture and bring to a boil over high heat, stirring. Serve sauce with chicken and rice. Makes 4 servings.

Per serving: 741 calories, 49 g protein, 81 g carbohydrates, 23 g fat, 6 g saturated fat, 143 mg cholesterol, 358 mg sodium

Clusters of sautéed chanterelles and fans of snow peas frame a platter of Hot & Sweet Chicken (recipe on facing page). The baked chicken pieces are basted and sauced with a tart, tempting blend of citrus juices, hot pepper, and currant jelly.

15

OVEN-BARBECUED CHICKEN

Preparation time: About 10 minutes

Cooking time: About 50 minutes

There's no need to light the grill to make this super-saucy chicken—you cook it right in your oven. Chili-sparked pineapple juice glazes and flavors the pieces as they bake.

- 3 tablespoons firmly packed brown sugar
- 1 tablespoon cornstarch
- ¾ cup pineapple juice
- 3 tablespoons catsup
- ¼ cup cider vinegar
- 1 tablespoon chili powder
- 1 teaspoon ground ginger
- ⅛ teaspoon ground allspice
- 1 tablespoon soy sauce
- 2 cloves garlic, minced or pressed
- 1 chicken (about 3½ lbs.), cut up

In a 1- to 1½-quart pan, mix sugar and cornstarch. Stir in pineapple juice, catsup, vinegar, chili powder, ginger, allspice, soy, and garlic. Bring to a boil over high heat, stirring. Remove from heat.

Rinse chicken and pat dry. Then arrange chicken, except breast pieces, skin side down in a foil-lined shallow 10- by 15-inch baking pan. Brush some of the sauce over chicken.

Bake, uncovered, in a 400° oven for 20 minutes. Turn chicken pieces over. Add breast pieces, skin side up, to pan; brush all chicken with remaining sauce. Continue to bake until skin is well browned and meat near thighbone is no longer pink; cut to test (about 25 more minutes). Makes 4 servings.

Per serving: 516 calories, 49 g protein, 24 g carbohydrates, 24 g fat, 7 g saturated fat, 154 mg cholesterol, 557 mg sodium

ROAST CHICKEN & FIGS

Preparation time: About 10 minutes

Cooking time: About 55 minutes

Sweet fresh figs complement roasted chicken quarters flavored with a simple orange juice and honey baste. You can use either black or green figs; both kinds are available in June and again from August until early September.

- 1 chicken (3 to 3½ lbs.), quartered
- 1 teaspoon grated orange peel
- ½ cup *each* orange juice and regular-strength chicken broth
- 1 tablespoon honey
- 12 large or 24 small ripe figs, stems trimmed

Rinse chicken, pat dry, and place, skin side up, in a shallow 12- by 15-inch roasting pan. Roast, uncovered, in a 375° oven for 40 minutes. Skim and discard fat from pan.

In a bowl, mix orange peel, orange juice, broth, and honey. Add figs; mix gently to coat.

With a slotted spoon, lift figs from bowl and spoon into pan alongside chicken. Then spoon juice mixture over chicken. Continue to roast until figs are hot and chicken meat near thighbone is no longer pink; cut to test (about 10 more minutes).

Spoon sauce from roasting pan into a 1- to 2-quart pan. Turn off oven; return roasting pan with chicken and figs to oven to keep warm. Boil sauce over high heat until reduced to ½ cup (about 3 minutes).

Divide chicken and figs equally among 4 dinner plates; top with sauce. Makes 4 servings.

Per serving: 564 calories, 46 g protein, 45 g carbohydrates, 23 g fat, 6 g saturated fat, 143 mg cholesterol, 259 mg sodium

CHICKEN-RICE-TOMATILLO BAKE

Preparation time: About 10 minutes

Cooking time: About 1 hour and 5 minutes

Chicken pieces bake on a rice pilaf with a difference: it's treated to tangy tomatillos, ground cumin, and cilantro. To accompany the dish, offer fresh corn on the cob coated with melted butter and sprinkled with cracked black pepper.

- 1 **chicken (about 3½ lbs.), cut up**
- 2 **tablespoons salad oil**
- 1 **medium-size onion, chopped**
- 1 **clove garlic, minced or pressed**
- 1 **cup long-grain white rice**
- 1 **can (18 oz.) tomatillos**
  About 1 cup regular-strength chicken broth
- 1 **can (4 oz.) whole green chiles, thinly sliced crosswise**
- 1 **teaspoon ground cumin**
- 2 **tablespoons minced fresh cilantro (coriander)**
  Cilantro (coriander) sprigs

Rinse chicken and pat dry. Heat oil in a 12- to 14-inch frying pan over medium-high heat. Add chicken pieces, a portion at a time; cook, turning as needed, until browned on all sides (about 6 minutes). Remove chicken from pan; set aside. Pour off and discard all but 2 tablespoons of the drippings.

Add onion, garlic, and rice to reserved drippings in pan; cook, stirring often, until rice is golden (about 5 minutes). Set aside.

Drain liquid from tomatillos and add enough of the broth to make 2 cups. Cut each tomatillo in half. In a 9- by 13-inch baking dish, mix broth mixture, tomatillos, chiles, cumin, minced cilantro, and rice mixture.

Arrange chicken, except breast pieces, skin side up atop rice. Bake, uncovered, in a 350° oven for 15 minutes. Add breast pieces and any accumulated juices. Continue to bake, uncovered, until meat near thighbone is no longer pink; cut to test (about 30 more minutes). Garnish with cilantro sprigs. Makes 4 servings.

Per serving: 717 calories, 53 g protein, 45 g carbohydrates, 35 g fat, 9 g saturated fat, 159 mg cholesterol, 717 mg sodium

CHICKEN SANTA FE

Preparation time: About 10 minutes

Cooking time: About 1¼ hours

Spicy yet not too hot, this dinner should please anyone with a taste for Southwest cooking. It features plenty of green chiles and just a touch of hot taco sauce; you can add more sauce to taste.

- 1 **large can (7 oz.) whole green chiles**
- 1 **chicken (about 3½ lbs.), cut up**
- 2 **slices bacon**
- 1 **large onion, cut into eighths**
- 2 **cloves garlic, minced or pressed**
- ½ **cup *each* dry white wine and regular-strength chicken broth**
- 1 **tablespoon prepared hot taco sauce**
- ¼ **teaspoon ground cumin**
  Salt and pepper

Dice half the chiles; cut remaining chiles lengthwise into thin strips. Set aside in separate piles. Rinse chicken, pat dry, and set aside.

Cook bacon in a 12- to 14-inch frying pan or 5- to 6-quart pan over medium heat until crisp. Lift out;

drain on paper towels. Increase heat under pan to medium-high. Add chicken pieces, a portion at a time, to bacon drippings; cook, turning as needed, until browned on all sides (about 6 minutes). Remove from pan and set aside. Pour off and discard all but 2 tablespoons of the drippings.

Add onion and garlic to reserved drippings in pan; cook, stirring often, until onion is soft and layers are separated. Crumble bacon; add to onion along with diced chiles, wine, broth, taco sauce, and cumin. Mix well. Add chicken and any accumulated juices to sauce, arranging chicken pieces skin side up. Spoon some of sauce up over chicken, then arrange chile strips over chicken.

Reduce heat, cover, and simmer until meat near thighbone is no longer pink; cut to test (about 30 minutes). With a slotted spoon, lift chicken from pan and place on a platter; keep warm. Boil sauce over high heat until reduced by about half. Spoon sauce around chicken. Season to taste with salt and pepper. Makes 4 servings.

Per serving: 679 calories, 53 g protein, 7 g carbohydrates, 48 g fat, 14 g saturated fat, 210 mg cholesterol, 799 mg sodium

The garnish tells the story: this dish is spicy! Browned chicken simmers with tomatoes, carrots, sweet currants, and fresh chiles to make a sensational stew. Serve Chicken with Currants & Jalapeños (recipe on facing page) with colorful accompaniments: corn with onion and red pepper, and a cool salad of apples, jicama, and pomegranate seeds in lime juice.

■ *Pictured on facing page*

CHICKEN WITH CURRANTS & JALAPEÑOS

Preparation time: About 10 minutes

Cooking time: About 1 hour and 5 minutes

Turn chicken stew from standard to sassy with the heated addition of fresh jalapeños. Dried currants add a sweet accent and soak up some of the spicy sauce.

- 1 **chicken (about 4 lbs.), cut up**
- ¾ **teaspoon paprika**
- 2 **tablespoons olive oil or salad oil**
- 5 **cloves garlic, minced or pressed**
- 2 **fresh jalapeño chiles, seeded and minced**
- 1 **large onion, chopped**
- 2 **medium-size carrots, sliced**
- 4 **ounces mushrooms, sliced**
- 1 **can (14½ oz.) stewed tomatoes**
- ½ **teaspoon ground cumin**
- ½ **teaspoon fines herbes or dry thyme leaves**
- ¾ **cup dry white wine or regular-strength chicken broth**
- ½ **cup dried currants**

Rinse chicken, pat dry, and sprinkle all over with paprika. Heat oil in a 4- to 5-quart pan over medium-high heat. Add chicken pieces, a portion at a time; cook, turning as needed, until browned on all sides (about 6 minutes). Remove from pan and set aside.

Add garlic, chiles, onion, and carrots to pan. Cook, stirring often, until vegetables begin to brown lightly (about 12 minutes). Add mushrooms, tomatoes, cumin, fines herbes, wine, and currants; then add chicken and any accumulated juices. Bring to a boil. Then reduce heat and simmer, uncovered, until meat near thighbone is no longer pink; cut to test (about 40 minutes). Makes 4 servings.

Per serving: 853 calories, 61 g protein, 31 g carbohydrates, 54 g fat, 14 g saturated fat, 232 mg cholesterol, 524 mg sodium

BRAISED CHICKEN WITH GARLIC, TOMATOES & POTATOES

Preparation time: About 15 minutes

Cooking time: About 55 minutes

Two *dozen* garlic cloves? That alarming number may be enough to make you flinch and promptly turn the page. But give this meal a try—you'll be surprised by its deliciously mellow flavor. The secret lies in cooking the cloves without cutting them.

- 1 **chicken (about 3½ lbs.), cut up**
- 2 **tablespoons salad oil**
- 24 **large cloves garlic, peeled**
- 4 **large firm-ripe pear-shaped tomatoes (about 12 oz. *total*), cut in half lengthwise**
- 1 **cup *each* dry white wine and regular-strength chicken broth**
- 4 **small thin-skinned potatoes (each 1½ to 2 inches in diameter), scrubbed and cut in half**
  Salt and pepper

Rinse chicken and pat dry. Heat oil in a 12- to 14-inch frying pan or 5- to 6-quart pan over medium-high heat. Add chicken pieces, a portion at a time; cook, turning as needed, until browned on all sides (about 6 minutes). Remove from pan and set aside.

Reduce heat to medium; add garlic and tomato halves, cut side down, to pan. Cook until tomatoes are lightly browned (about 2 minutes). Lift out tomatoes; set aside.

Add chicken and any accumulated juices to pan, then add wine, broth, and potatoes. Bring to a boil; then reduce heat, cover, and simmer until potatoes are tender when pierced (about 25 minutes). Set tomatoes on top of chicken. Continue to simmer, covered, until meat near thighbone is no longer pink; cut to test (about 5 more minutes). With a slotted spoon, lift out chicken, garlic, potatoes, and tomatoes; place on a platter and keep warm.

Boil pan juices over high heat until reduced to about 1 cup (about 5 minutes). Pour over chicken. Season to taste with salt and pepper. Makes 4 servings.

Per serving: 742 calories, 54 g protein, 21 g carbohydrates, 78 g fat, 13 g saturated fat, 203 mg cholesterol, 453 mg sodium

COOK'S CHOICE—CHICKEN OR TURKEY

Today's markets offer a wide selection of skinless, boneless cuts of chicken and turkey—and that presents plenty of options for creative cooks. You'll be able to devise all sorts of appetizing recipes, many of them low in fat and quick to cook. With appropriate attention to preparation, it's even possible to interchange chicken and turkey in some dishes. Such a substitution is easiest for ground meat (see pages 90 to 109), but on these two pages, we offer suggestions for roasting, steeping, barbecuing, and stir-frying chicken or turkey breasts, thighs, or tenderloins.

Note: We used chicken breast to calculate our preparation times, cooking times, and nutritional data.

ROASTED THAI NUGGETS

Preparation time: About 15 minutes

Roasting time: About 12 minutes

    Thai Sauce (page 105)
1 pound skinless, boneless chicken or turkey
3 tablespoons minced fresh cilantro (coriander)
2 teaspoons coarsely ground pepper
6 cloves garlic, minced

Prepare Thai Sauce and refrigerate.

Rinse poultry and pat dry. *If using chicken breast halves,* cut each diagonally across the grain into 2 equal pieces; tuck thin ends under. *If using chicken thighs,* roll each into a compact shape. *If using turkey breast or thigh,* cut into 8 equal-size pieces no thicker than 1½ inches. *If using turkey tenderloins,* split lengthwise, cutting away tendon in center; divide into 8 equal-size pieces.

Mix cilantro, pepper, and garlic. Rub mixture over poultry, then place pieces well apart in an ungreased shallow 10- by 15-inch baking pan.

Roast, uncovered, in a 500° oven until meat is lightly browned and no longer pink in center; cut to test. Allow about 12 minutes for chicken breast, 18 minutes for chicken thigh, 10 minutes for turkey breast or ten-

derloin, and 15 minutes for turkey thigh. Serve with Thai Sauce. Makes 4 servings.

Per serving without sauce: 134 calories, 27 g protein, 2 g carbohydrates, 1 g fat, 0 g saturated fat, 66 mg cholesterol, 75 mg sodium

STEEPED POULTRY IN ROLLS

Preparation time: About 15 minutes

Cooking time: About 25 minutes

1 pound skinless, boneless chicken or turkey
4 cups water
2 cups regular-strength chicken broth
¼ cup chili powder
¼ cup firmly packed brown sugar
2 teaspoons dry oregano leaves
1 star anise or 1 teaspoon anise seeds
3 tablespoons *each* olive oil and red wine vinegar
2 tablespoons *each* chopped fresh cilantro (coriander) and minced green onion (including top)
4 French rolls (*each* 6 inches long), split
    Butter lettuce leaves, washed and crisped

Rinse poultry and pat dry. Place all pieces to be pounded between 2 sheets of plastic wrap. *If using chicken breast halves or thighs,* cook as is. *If using a 1-pound turkey breast piece,* cut across the grain into 1-inch-thick slices. *If using turkey tenderloins or turkey thigh,* pound with a flat-surfaced mallet until ½ to ¾ inch thick.

In a 4- to 5-quart pan with a tight-fitting lid, combine water, broth, chili powder, sugar, oregano, and anise; bring to a boil. Remove from heat and immediately add poultry pieces, opened out as flat as possible. Cover pan and let stand until meat is no longer pink in center; lift from water and cut to test (do not lift cover until ready to test). Allow about 20 minutes for all poultry cuts; if meat is not done, return to water, cover, and let steep for about 2 more minutes.

Drain meat, reserving 2 cups of the steeping liquid. Boil reserved 2 cups liquid over high heat until reduced to ⅓ cup; as liquid becomes concentrated, watch carefully to prevent scorching. Serve meat warm; or, to serve cold, cover meat and liquid separately and refrigerate for up to 2 days.

To serve, prepare a dressing by mixing reduced liquid with oil, vinegar, cilantro, and onion. Cut poultry pieces across the grain into thin, slanting slices. Moisten cut surfaces of rolls with dressing; fill rolls with meat and lettuce. Makes 4 servings.

Per serving: 414 calories, 32 g protein, 39 g carbohydrates, 14 g fat, 2 g saturated fat, 68 mg cholesterol, 596 mg sodium

GRILLED ROMAINE WRAPS

Preparation time: About 15 minutes

Grilling time: About 20 minutes

Green Dressing (recipe follows)
1 pound skinless, boneless chicken or turkey
2 large, 4 medium-size, or 8 small romaine lettuce leaves (size depends on poultry used; see instructions below)
4 thin slices prosciutto (about 2½ oz. total)
Salt and pepper

Prepare Green Dressing and set aside. Rinse poultry and pat dry; set aside.

In a 10- to 12-inch frying pan, bring 1 inch water to a boil. Plunge lettuce into water for 1 minute. Lift out; immerse in cold water until cool. Drain and pat dry.

If using chicken breast halves, wrap each piece in 1 slice prosciutto and 1 medium-size lettuce leaf. *If using chicken thighs,* roll each into a compact shape and wrap in a half-slice of prosciutto and 1 small lettuce leaf. *If using a 1-pound turkey breast piece or thigh,* cut into 4 equal-size logs (each 1 to 1½ inches thick); wrap each in 1 slice prosciutto and 1 medium-size lettuce leaf. *If using large turkey tenderloins,* wrap each in 2 slices prosciutto and 1 large lettuce leaf.

Place wrapped poultry on a grill 4 to 6 inches above a solid bed of medium coals. Cook, turning occasionally, until meat in thickest part is no longer pink; cut to test. Allow about 20 minutes for chicken or turkey breast, about 25 minutes for turkey tenderloin, chicken thigh, or turkey thigh.

To serve, cut meat across the grain into 1-inch-thick slices; arrange on 4 dinner plates. Add Green Dressing, salt, and pepper to taste. Makes 4 servings.

Per serving without dressing: 160 calories, 31 g protein, 0 g carbohydrates, 3 g fat, 1 g saturated fat, 76 mg cholesterol, 342 mg sodium

GREEN DRESSING. In a blender or food processor, combine ⅓ cup **olive oil** or salad oil, ¼ cup **white wine vinegar,** 2 tablespoons minced **onion,** 1 tablespoon minced **parsley,** and 2 teaspoons *each* minced **fresh sage and thyme leaves** (or ¾ teaspoon *each* dry leaves). Whirl until puréed. Makes ½ cup.

Per tablespoon: 81 calories, 0 g protein, 1 g carbohydrates, 9 g fat, 1 g saturated fat, 0 mg cholesterol, 0 mg sodium

STIR-FRIED POULTRY

Preparation time: About 15 minutes

Cooking time: About 6 minutes

1 pound skinless, boneless chicken or turkey
¾ cup regular-strength chicken broth
1 tablespoon lemon juice
2 tablespoons drained capers
2 to 3 tablespoons olive oil or salad oil
1 small onion, cut into 1-inch squares
About 4 cups washed, crisped arugula, watercress, or Belgian endive

Rinse poultry and pat dry. Place all pieces to be pounded between 2 sheets of plastic wrap. *If using chicken or turkey stir-fry strips or chicken tenderloins,* cook as is. *If using chicken breast halves, chicken thighs, or turkey breast slices,* pound with a flat-surfaced mallet until about ¼ inch thick. *If using turkey tenderloins,* split lengthwise, cutting away tendon in center; then cut across the grain into ¼-inch-thick slices. *If using turkey thigh,* cut across the grain into ¼-inch-thick slices. Cut all larger poultry pieces into 1-inch squares.

To prepare sauce, mix broth, lemon juice, and capers in a small bowl. Set aside.

Heat 1 tablespoon of the oil in a 12- to 14-inch frying pan or wok over high heat. Add onion; cook, stirring, until browned at edges (about 2 minutes). Pour onion into a bowl. Add 1 more tablespoon oil to pan; then add half the poultry in a single layer. Cook until meat begins to brown (about 1 minute). Then turn pieces over and continue to cook until no longer pink in center; cut to test (about 30 more seconds). Add to onion in bowl. Repeat to cook remaining poultry, adding more oil if needed to prevent sticking.

Pour sauce into pan, stir to scrape up browned bits, and boil until reduced to ¼ cup. Remove pan from heat and stir in poultry mixture. Distribute greens equally on 4 dinner plates; spoon poultry mixture over greens. Makes 4 servings.

Per serving: 212 calories, 28 g protein, 2 g carbohydrates, 10 g fat, 2 g saturated fat, 66 mg cholesterol, 384 mg sodium

CHILI-GLAZED CHICKEN WITH PEAS

Preparation time: About 5 minutes

Grilling time: About 40 minutes

Try serving iced tea and margaritas with this lime-
and chili-charged chicken. A buttery baste helps keep
the pieces moist—and makes them especially flavorful, too.

- 1 **chicken (3 to 3½ lbs.), cut up**
- ⅓ **cup butter or margarine, melted**
- 2 **cloves garlic, minced or pressed**
- 1 **teaspoon chili powder**
- ¼ **teaspoon *each* ground cumin and grated lime peel**
- 2 **tablespoons lime juice**
- 2 **pounds peas in the pod**
- 2 **tablespoons water**

Rinse chicken and pat dry. In a small pan, stir
together butter, garlic, chili powder, cumin, lime
peel, and lime juice. Brush generously over chicken.

Arrange chicken, except breast pieces, skin side
up on a lightly greased grill 4 to 6 inches above a solid
bed of medium coals. Cook for 15 minutes, turning
and basting frequently with butter mixture. Place
breast pieces on grill. Continue to cook, turning and
basting often, until meat near thighbone is no longer
pink; cut to test (about 25 more minutes).

Meanwhile, rinse peas; then place in a cast-iron
frying pan or Dutch oven and add water. Cover with
lid or foil; place on grill next to chicken during last 15
minutes of cooking, stirring peas every 5 minutes. Let
guests shell their own peas to eat alongside chicken.
Makes 4 servings.

*Per serving: 599 calories, 49 g protein, 14 g carbohydrates,
38 g fat, 16 g saturated fat, 184 mg cholesterol, 299 mg sodium*

BARBECUED TURKEY

Preparation time: 15 minutes, plus 30 minutes to heat coals

Grilling time: 4 to 4½ hours

It's easy to roast a big turkey out on the patio if you
grill it by indirect heat in a covered barbecue. Fresh
rosemary sprigs on the hot coals add an appealing
aroma to the barbecued bird.

- 1 **turkey (20 to 22 lbs.)**
- 2 **teaspoons poultry seasoning**
- ¼ **teaspoon pepper**
- 1 **cup port**
- 1 **large onion, quartered**
- 2 **large carrots (about 12 oz. *total*), cut into chunks**
- 2 **stalks celery, cut into chunks**
- 1 **clove garlic, quartered**
- 3 **or 4 rosemary sprigs (*each* 3 to 4 inches long)**

Open or remove lid from a covered barbecue;
open bottom dampers. Pile about 50 long-burning
briquets on fire grate and ignite them. Let briquets
burn until hot (about 30 minutes). Using long-
handled tongs, bank about half the briquets on each
side of fire grate; then place a metal drip pan in center. Set cooking grill in place 4 to 6 inches above
pan; lightly grease grill.

Reserve turkey neck and giblets for other uses; pull
off and discard lumps of fat from turkey. Rinse turkey
inside and out; pat dry. Combine poultry seasoning
and pepper. Sprinkle some of mixture into neck and
body cavities; rub remaining mixture over skin. Place
turkey on its breast and spoon 1 to 2 tablespoons of
the port into neck cavity; bring skin over opening and
skewer cavity shut. Turn turkey on its back and place
onion, carrots, celery, and garlic in body cavity.

Place turkey, breast up, on grill directly above drip
pan. Pour about ⅓ cup of the remaining port into body
cavity; cover barbecue and adjust dampers as necessary to maintain an even heat. Cook until a meat thermometer, inserted straight down through thickest part
of breast until it touches the bone, registers 160°F; or
cook until meat near thighbone is no longer pink (cut
to test). Total time will be 4 to 4½ hours.

Several times during cooking, place a rosemary
sprig on the coals to add fragrance as it smolders.
During last hour, brush turkey with port several
times, using all remaining port. When turkey is done,
discard stuffing. Makes 16 to 18 servings.

*Per serving: 448 calories, 77 g protein, 1 g carbohydrates,
12 g fat, 4 g saturated fat, 202 mg cholesterol, 197 mg sodium*

Keep company busy at your next barbecue with our Chili-glazed Chicken with Peas (recipe on facing page). Between bites of spicy butter-basted chicken, guests shell and enjoy fresh peas steamed in a kettle on the grill.

Preparation time: About 1½ hours

Cooking time: 3¼ to 3¾ hours

When it comes to roast turkey, doubling the pleasure means doubling the opportunity to eat stuffing! This plump bird is sure to please; it's filled with a richly seasoned wild rice stuffing, while a lighter brown rice dressing bakes alongside.

> **Wild & Tame Rice Stuffings (recipe follows)**
> **Brown Turkey Gravy (recipe on facing page)**
> 1 **turkey (12 to 14 lbs.)**
> **About 3 tablespoons olive oil**
> **Parsley, rosemary, or thyme sprigs**

Prepare Wild & Tame Rice Stuffings; set aside.

Reserve turkey neck for other uses. Rinse turkey giblets; begin preparing Brown Turkey Gravy.

Pull off and discard lumps of fat from turkey. Rinse turkey inside and out, pat dry, and fill breast and body cavities with wild rice–chard stuffing. Skewer cavities shut. Rub bird all over with oil; then place, breast down, on a V-shaped rack set in a 12- by 15-inch roasting pan.

Roast, uncovered, in a 350° oven for 1 hour; remove from oven. Tilt bird to drain juices into pan; then turn breast up. Continue to roast until a meat thermometer, inserted straight down through thickest part of breast until it touches the bone, registers 160°F; or roast until meat near thighbone is no longer pink (cut to test). Additional time will be 2 to 2½ hours.

About 1 hour before turkey is done, place brown rice–spinach stuffing in a greased shallow 2- to 2½-quart baking dish. Cover tightly and bake until very hot in center (about 1 hour).

Remove skewers from turkey; spoon stuffing into a wide, shallow serving bowl, mounding it on one side.

Mound brown rice–spinach stuffing in bowl on other side. Place turkey on a platter. Keep turkey and stuffing warm while you finish gravy. Garnish turkey and stuffing with herbs; offer gravy to spoon over meat and stuffing. Makes 8 to 12 servings.

Per serving turkey without dressing or gravy: 488 calories, 85 g protein, 0 g carbohydrates, 14 g fat, 4 g saturated fat, 224 mg cholesterol, 215 mg sodium

WILD & TAME RICE STUFFINGS. In a 1- to 2-quart pan, bring 1½ cups **water** to a boil over high heat. Add ½ cup **wild rice,** rinsed and drained. Also, in a 3- to 4-quart pan, bring 3 cups **water** to a boil over high heat; add 1¾ cups **long-grain brown rice.** Reduce heat under both pans, cover, and simmer until rices are tender to bite (about 45 minutes). Drain.

While rices are cooking, place 1½ ounces **dried porcini mushrooms** (cèpes) in a bowl and add 1⅓ cups **hot water.** Let stand until mushrooms are limp (about 20 minutes), then gently squeeze mushrooms in the water to help release any grit. Lift out mushrooms, chop, and set aside. Pour soaking liquid into another container, taking care not to disturb residue in bottom of bowl. Save liquid for gravy; discard residue.

Place two 10- to 12-inch frying pans over medium-high heat. Into one pan, crumble ⅓ pound **hot Italian sausage** (casings removed); into other pan, crumble ⅓ pound **mild Italian sausage** (casings removed). Cook, stirring often to break sausage into small bits, until lightly browned (about 5 minutes). With a slotted spoon, transfer to paper towels to drain; then place each kind of sausage in a separate large bowl.

To each frying pan, add 2 tablespoons **olive oil** or salad oil and 1 medium-size **onion,** chopped.

To pan in which hot sausage was cooked, also add porcini mushrooms; 4 ounces **button mushrooms,** sliced; 3 cloves **garlic,** minced or pressed; and 1½ to 2 tablespoons *each* minced **fresh marjoram leaves** and minced **fresh sage** (or about 2 teaspoons *each* dry leaves). To other frying pan, add 1½ tablespoons *each* minced **fresh marjoram leaves** and minced **fresh sage** (or about 2 teaspoons *each* dry leaves) and 1¼ cups sliced **celery.** Cook, stirring often, until vegetables in both pans are very soft (about 10 minutes).

Meanwhile, rinse 8 ounces **Swiss chard;** drain and chop. Also remove stems and any wilted leaves from 12 ounces **spinach;** rinse remaining leaves, drain, and chop.

Add chard to pan with mushrooms, spinach to pan with celery. Cook, stirring often, until greens are wilted and liquid has evaporated (4 to 6 minutes).

To bowl with hot sausage, add chard mixture, wild rice, 2 cups of the brown rice, ½ cup grated **Parmesan cheese,** and ½ cup **dry white wine.** To bowl with mild sausage, add spinach mixture, remaining brown rice, ½ cup grated **Parmesan cheese,** ¼ cup **dry white wine,** and ½ cup **regular-strength chicken broth.** Mix contents of both bowls well; season to taste with **salt** and **pepper.** If made ahead, cover and refrigerate for up to 1 day. Makes 12 cups.

Per ½ cup of wild rice–chard stuffing: 153 calories, 6 g protein, 16 g carbohydrates, 8 g fat, 3 g saturated fat, 12 mg cholesterol, 196 mg sodium

Per ½ cup of brown rice–spinach stuffing: 154 calories, 6 g protein, 16 g carbohydrates, 8 g fat, 3 g saturated fat, 12 mg cholesterol, 218 mg sodium

BROWN TURKEY GRAVY. Wrap and refrigerate **turkey liver;** place remaining **turkey giblets** in a 3- to 4-quart pan. Add 1 medium-size **onion,** quartered; 1 large stalk **celery,** chopped; 2 **dry bay leaves;** ½ teaspoon **dry thyme leaves;** 5 cups **water;** and **soaking liquid from porcini mushrooms** (reserved from stuffing).

Bring to a boil over high heat; then reduce heat, cover, and simmer until gizzard is very tender when pierced (about 2¼ hours). Add liver to pan; simmer for 15 more minutes.

Pour broth through a fine strainer; discard vegetables and giblets. Measure broth; you should have 5 cups. If necessary, boil broth over high heat to reduce; or add **regular-strength chicken broth** to increase amount. Return strained broth to cooking pan.

After turkey is done, pour fat and drippings from roasting pan into a glass measuring cup. Let stand until fat rises to surface, then ladle out and discard all but ¼ cup of the fat. Add this reserved fat and drippings to roasting pan; stir or whisk over medium-high heat, scraping up browned bits. Then scrape mixture into pan of broth.

In a small bowl, stir together ½ cup **cornstarch** and 1 cup **dry white wine** or regular-strength chicken broth until smooth. Add to broth in pan. Bring to a boil over high heat, whisking or stirring constantly. Pour into a bowl or gravy boat. Makes 6 cups.

Per tablespoon: 11 calories, 0 g protein, 1 g carbohydrates, 1 g fat, 0 g saturated fat, 2 mg cholesterol, 1 mg sodium

BLACK BEAN TURKEY CASSOULET

Preparation time: About 25 minutes

Cooking time: About 3¼ hours

Cassoulet is traditionally prepared with goose or duck and white beans, but our version—made with black beans and turkey pieces—is every bit as satisfying and hearty. It's the perfect meal for winter parties; just add a tossed salad and dark beer.

- 3 **large onions**
- 4 **ounces sliced bacon, chopped**
- 2 **parsley sprigs**
- 2 **dry bay leaves**
- 2 **teaspoons dry thyme leaves**
- 4 **cloves garlic, minced or pressed**
- 1½ **pounds dried black beans**
- 2 **pounds boneless pork shoulder or butt (trimmed of excess fat), cut into 1-inch chunks**
- 6 **cups regular-strength chicken broth**
- 1 **small turkey (about 8 lbs.), cut up**
- 1 **pound garlic sausages**
- ½ **cup (¼ lb.) butter or margarine**
- 2 **cups coarse soft bread crumbs**

Coarsely chop one of the onions; place in a 7- to 8-quart pan and add bacon. Cook over medium-high heat, stirring often, until onion is soft (about 7 minutes). Add parsley, bay leaves, thyme, and half the garlic; cook, stirring often, until garlic is soft (about 2 minutes). Remove from heat.

Sort beans and discard any debris. Rinse beans well, drain, and add to onion mixture along with pork; then stir in broth. Bring to a boil; reduce heat, cover, and simmer, stirring occasionally, until beans mash easily (about 2½ hours).

Meanwhile, place remaining 2 onions (unpeeled) in a shallow baking pan. Bake, uncovered, in a 350° oven until soft when pressed (about 1½ hours). Let cool; peel and cut lengthwise into quarters.

Also rinse turkey and pat dry. Then arrange turkey (skin side up) and sausages in a single layer in a shallow 10- by 15-inch baking pan. Bake, uncovered, in a 350° oven until meat near turkey thighbone is no longer pink; cut to test (about 50 minutes; turn meats after 30 minutes). Remove meats from pan with a slotted spoon; cut sausages into ¼-inch-thick diagonal slices.

Melt butter in a 10- to 12-inch frying pan over medium-high heat. Add crumbs and remaining garlic; stir until crumbs are light brown (about 3 minutes).

Divide bean mixture between two 4-quart casseroles; mix half each of the onions, turkey pieces, and sausages into each. Sprinkle evenly with crumbs. Bake, uncovered, in a 350° oven until hot and golden brown on top (about 30 minutes). Makes 16 servings.

Per serving: 762 calories, 64 g protein, 33 g carbohydrates, 41 g fat, 15 g saturated fat, 210 mg cholesterol, 865 mg sodium

*For a meal that's simple to prepare and simply delicious,
serve steamed baby bok choy and red potatoes alongside Baked
Chicken Breasts with Pears (recipe on page 28). You poach the fruit in
pear brandy while the soy-coated chicken breasts bake.*

Tender Breast Meat

BUNDLED & BREADED & FRUITED & CHEESED &

SAUTÉED & CHUTNEYED & STEAMED & SMOKED &

CREAMED & ROLLED & GINGERED & BROILED &

STEWED & SCENTED & KEBABED & SLICED &

HERB-BAKED CHICKEN BREASTS

Preparation time: About 10 minutes

Marinating time: At least 1 hour or up to 1 day

Cooking time: About 1 hour and 10 minutes

A simple marinade accented with thyme and rosemary dresses up chicken breasts for Sunday supper. Onions and bright bell peppers bake alongside the chicken; you might round out the meal with a bowl of fluffy mashed potatoes.

> 6 **skinless, boneless chicken breast halves (about 1½ lbs. *total*)**
> **Herb Marinade (recipe follows)**
> 2 **large onions, sliced crosswise**
> 2 *each* **large red and yellow bell peppers (1½ to 2 lbs. *total*), seeded and slivered**
> 3 **tablespoons olive oil**
> ½ **cup *each* regular-strength chicken broth and dry red wine**

Rinse chicken, pat dry, and place, skinned side up, in a shallow 10- by 15-inch baking pan. Prepare Herb Marinade; brush over chicken. Cover and refrigerate for at least 1 hour or up to 1 day.

Place onions and bell peppers in a 12- by 17-inch baking pan; drizzle evenly with oil. Bake, uncovered, on lower rack of a 450° oven for 45 minutes, stirring occasionally. Place pan of chicken on upper rack of oven. Continue to bake, stirring vegetables occasionally, for about 20 more minutes. Vegetables should be soft when pierced and browned at edges; chicken meat in thickest part should no longer be pink (cut to test). With a slotted spoon, transfer onions, peppers, and chicken to a platter; cover and keep warm.

Skim any fat from chicken pan juices; add broth and wine. Boil over high heat, stirring to scrape up browned bits, until reduced to ½ cup (about 5 minutes). Spoon sauce over chicken. Makes 6 servings.

HERB MARINADE. In a small bowl, stir together 3 tablespoons **olive oil**, 1 tablespoon **balsamic vinegar** or red wine vinegar, 1½ teaspoons *each* **dry rosemary** and **dry thyme leaves,** and ¼ teaspoon coarsely ground **pepper.**

Per serving: 296 calories, 28 g protein, 11 g carbohydrates, 16 g fat, 2 g saturated fat, 66 mg cholesterol, 162 mg sodium

■ *Pictured on page 26*

BAKED CHICKEN BREASTS WITH PEARS

Preparation time: About 5 minutes

Cooking time: About 20 minutes

Chicken breasts, a little soy sauce, some sliced pears—the dish may sound too plain, but wait until you taste it! These aren't just any pears; they're first poached in fragrant brandy, then tossed with the meat and pan juices to make a memorable meal.

> 6 **skinless, boneless chicken breast halves (about 1½ lbs. *total*)**
> 3 **tablespoons soy sauce**
> 4 **teaspoons cornstarch**
> 1 **cup pear-flavored brandy or apple juice**
> 2 **medium-size firm-ripe pears**
> **Parsley sprigs**
> **Salt and pepper**
> **Lime wedges**

Rinse chicken and pat dry; then arrange, skinned side up, in a 9- by 13-inch baking pan. Drizzle

evenly with soy. Bake, uncovered, in a 450° oven, basting occasionally, until meat in thickest part is no longer pink; cut to test (about 20 minutes).

Meanwhile, place cornstarch in a 1½- to 2-quart pan; smoothly stir in brandy. Peel and core pears, then cut lengthwise into ½-inch-thick slices. Add pears to pan and bring to a boil over medium-high heat, mixing gently. Then reduce heat, cover, and simmer until pears are tender when pierced (about 5 minutes).

When chicken is done, add pear mixture to baking pan; gently shake pan to mix pears and chicken. Transfer chicken, pears, and sauce to a platter and garnish with parsley. Season to taste with salt and pepper; offer lime wedges to squeeze over individual servings. Makes 6 servings.

Per serving: 248 calories, 27 g protein, 23 g carbohydrates, 2 g fat, 0 g saturated fat, 66 mg cholesterol, 588 mg sodium

PLUM CHICKEN

Preparation time: About 10 minutes

Baking time: About 25 minutes

"Spicy" and "succulent" are the words that describe this quick-to-cook entrée. Bottled plum sauce sparked with ginger and anise glazes the juicy chicken. Serve with brown rice and a green vegetable—perhaps snap beans, snow peas, or broccoli.

- **4** **skinless, boneless chicken breast halves (about 1 lb. *total*)**
- **1** **cup Oriental plum sauce**
- **¼** **cup minced onion**
- **2** **tablespoons lemon juice**
- **1** **tablespoon reduced-sodium soy sauce**
- **1** **teaspoon grated lemon peel**
- **½** **teaspoon *each* dry mustard and ground ginger**
- **¼** **teaspoon *each* pepper and liquid hot pepper seasoning**
- **¼** **teaspoon anise seeds, crushed**

Rinse chicken, pat dry, and place, skinned side up, in a 9- by 13-inch or other shallow 3-quart baking dish. In a small bowl, stir together plum sauce, onion, lemon juice, soy, lemon peel, mustard, ginger, pepper, hot pepper seasoning, and anise seeds. Pour over chicken.

Bake chicken, uncovered, in a 400° oven until meat in thickest part is no longer pink; cut to test (about 25 minutes). Baste chicken halfway through baking. To serve, transfer chicken to a platter; spoon sauce on top. Makes 4 servings.

Per serving: 353 calories, 27 g protein, 58 g carbohydrates, 2 g fat, 0 g saturated fat, 66 mg cholesterol, 243 mg sodium

DIJON BAKED CHICKEN

Preparation time: About 20 minutes

Baking time: About 25 minutes

When only the best will do, choose this recipe. Boneless breast halves are coated with white wine and Dijon mustard, rolled in fresh bread crumbs seasoned with parsley and Parmesan, and baked until golden. Serve hot; or chill, then serve cold for an elegant picnic entrée.

- **2** **cups soft bread crumbs**
- **½** **cup grated Parmesan cheese**
- **¼** **cup chopped parsley**
- **½** **cup (¼ lb.) butter or margarine, melted**
- **⅛** **teaspoon ground red pepper (cayenne)**
- **½** **cup Dijon mustard**
- **¼** **cup dry white wine**
- **2** **tablespoons minced shallots**
- **1** **teaspoon dry thyme leaves**
- **8** **skinless, boneless chicken breast halves (about 2 lbs. *total*)**

In a shallow pan or wide, shallow rimmed plate, combine crumbs, cheese, parsley, butter, and red pepper. In another shallow pan, mix mustard, wine, shallots, and thyme.

Rinse chicken and pat dry; coat with mustard mixture, then dip in crumb mixture. Arrange chicken pieces slightly apart in a greased shallow baking pan. Bake, uncovered, in a 400° oven until chicken is golden brown on outside and meat in thickest part is no longer pink; cut to test (about 25 minutes). Makes 8 servings.

Per serving: 302 calories, 30 g protein, 9 g carbohydrates, 16 g fat, 9 g saturated fat, 101 mg cholesterol, 791 mg sodium

EASY OVEN-FRIED CHICKEN

Preparation time: About 10 minutes

Marinating time: About 20 minutes

Baking time: About 20 minutes

Looking for an alternative to fried chicken? Baking is easier on the cook and more healthful for the diner. A little cornmeal adds an appealing crunch to the well-seasoned coating for these tender chicken breasts.

> 4 **skinless, boneless chicken breast halves (about 1 lb. *total*)**
>
> 2 **tablespoons dry sherry**
>
> 2 **cloves garlic, minced or pressed**
>
> ½ **cup soft whole wheat bread crumbs**
>
> 2 **tablespoons cornmeal**
>
> ½ **teaspoon salt**
>
> 1 **teaspoon paprika**
>
> ½ **teaspoon *each* pepper, dry sage leaves, dry thyme leaves, and dry basil leaves**
>
> 1 **teaspoon salad oil**

Rinse chicken and pat dry. In a shallow bowl, combine sherry and garlic. Add chicken, turn to coat, and let stand for about 20 minutes.

In a wide, shallow rimmed plate, combine crumbs, cornmeal, salt, paprika, pepper, sage, thyme, and basil. Dip each chicken piece in crumb mixture to coat.

Brush a shallow 10- by 15-inch baking pan with oil. Arrange chicken in pan. Bake, uncovered, in a 450° oven until meat in thickest part is no longer pink; cut to test (about 20 minutes). Serve hot or cold. Makes 4 servings.

Per serving: 175 calories, 27 g protein, 8 g carbohydrates, 3 g fat, 1 g saturated fat, 66 mg cholesterol, 382 mg sodium

■ *Pictured on facing page*

CHICKEN BREASTS WITH CHEESE & CHILES

Preparation time: About 10 minutes

Baking and broiling time: About 32 minutes

Piled high with creamy avocado, crisp bacon, and melted jack cheese, these chicken breasts offer a sensational medley of tastes and textures.

> 4 **skinless, boneless chicken breast halves (about 1 lb. *total*)**
>
> 1 **cup (4 oz.) shredded jack cheese**
>
> 1 **can (4 oz.) diced green chiles**
>
> ½ **cup chopped green onions (including tops)**
>
> 4 **slices bacon, crisply cooked, drained, and crumbled**
>
> 1 **medium-size firm-ripe avocado**
>
> 1 **cup sour cream (optional)**

Rinse chicken, pat dry, and place, skinned side up, in an 8- by 12-inch baking pan. Cover tightly with foil and bake in a 350° oven for 15 minutes. Meanwhile, mix cheese and chiles.

After chicken has baked for 15 minutes, remove foil. Top each piece equally with cheese mixture, patting to hold in place. Sprinkle evenly with onions and bacon.

Return to oven and continue to bake, uncovered, until cheese is melted and meat in thickest part is no longer pink; cut to test (about 15 more minutes). Then broil about 4 inches below heat until lightly browned (about 2 minutes).

Pit avocado, then peel and slice. To serve, arrange avocado over chicken; serve with sour cream, if desired. Makes 4 servings.

Per serving: 358 calories, 37 g protein, 6 g carbohydrates, 21 g fat, 3 g saturated fat, 96 mg cholesterol, 505 mg sodium

Here's a way to have supper in the Southwest without even leaving home. Corn sticks, black bean salad, baked papaya with lime juice, and icy sangrita are just the right partners for avocado-topped Chicken Breasts with Cheese & Chiles (recipe on facing page).

MACADAMIA CHICKEN

Preparation time: About 10 minutes

Cooking time: About 20 minutes

For a hint of Hawaii, serve up honey-sweetened chicken and fresh pineapple with a macadamia nut topping. Cooked spinach makes a colorful bed for the meat and fruit.

    4 **skinless, boneless chicken breast halves (about 1 lb. *total*)**

    1 **piece pineapple (about 2 lbs.), peeled, cored, and cut crosswise into 4 equal slices (weight of peeled pineapple will be about 1 lb.)**

    ¼ **cup Dijon mustard**

    3 **tablespoons honey**

    1 **tablespoon *each* salad oil and lime juice**

    2 **packages (10 oz. *each*) frozen chopped spinach**

    2 **tablespoons chopped salted macadamia nuts**

       Salt and pepper

Rinse chicken and pat dry. Place chicken (skinned side up) and pineapple side by side on rack of a 12- by 14-inch broiling pan. In a bowl, mix mustard, honey, oil, and lime juice; spoon half the mixture evenly over chicken and pineapple. Bake, uncovered, in a 450° oven until meat in thickest part is no longer pink; cut to test (about 20 minutes).

Meanwhile, cook spinach according to package directions; keep warm. Also warm remaining mustard mixture in a small pan over high heat.

To serve, place spinach on a platter, top with chicken and pineapple, and drizzle with mustard mixture. Sprinkle with macadamias and season to taste with salt and pepper. Makes 4 servings.

Per serving: 341 calories, 31 g protein, 36 g carbohydrates, 10 g fat, 1 g saturated fat, 66 mg cholesterol, 649 mg sodium

MELTDOWN CHICKEN BUNDLES

Preparation time: About 35 minutes

Baking time: About 20 minutes

Tucked inside rolled chicken breasts is an appetizing surprise: jalapeños and jack cheese. Fine bread crumbs blended with Parmesan cheese and chili powder make a crisp, golden coating for the baked bundles.

    8 **skinless, boneless chicken breast halves (about 2 lbs. *total*)**

    4 **pickled jalapeño chiles**

    4 **ounces jack cheese**

    ¼ **cup fine dry bread crumbs**

    2 **tablespoons grated Parmesan cheese**

    1 **teaspoon chili powder**

    ¼ **teaspoon *each* ground cumin and pepper**

    6 **tablespoons butter or margarine, melted**

Rinse chicken and pat dry. Place each breast half between 2 sheets of wax paper; pound with a flat-surfaced mallet to a thickness of about ¼ inch. Set chicken aside.

Stem and seed jalapeños, then cut each jalapeño lengthwise into ¼-inch-wide strips. Cut jack cheese into 8 equal strips.

In a wide, shallow rimmed plate, combine crumbs, Parmesan cheese, chili powder, cumin, and pepper.

To assemble each chicken bundle, place a strip of cheese and an eighth of the jalapeños on a pounded chicken breast half. Roll chicken around filling to enclose; coat roll with butter, then with crumb mixture.

Arrange rolls, seam side down, in a shallow 10- by 15-inch baking pan. Drizzle evenly with any remaining butter. Bake, uncovered, in a 425° oven until meat is no longer pink and filling is hot in center; cut to test (about 20 minutes). Makes 8 servings.

Per serving: 275 calories, 31 g protein, 3 g carbohydrates, 15 g fat, 6 g saturated fat, 103 mg cholesterol, 397 mg sodium

BROCCOLI-STUFFED CHICKEN BREASTS

Preparation time: About 45 minutes

Baking and broiling time: About 17 minutes

Top these chicken rolls with Swiss cheese and slip them under the broiler just until lightly browned; then let guests cut the golden bundles open to reveal the bright green broccoli-mushroom stuffing inside.

- 1 **tablespoon salad oil**
- ½ **cup minced shallots**
- 1 **pound mushrooms, minced**
- 2 **cups broccoli flowerets**
- 2 **tablespoons Madeira**
- 2 **tablespoons grated Parmesan cheese**
- ½ **cup shredded Swiss cheese**
- 6 **skinless, boneless chicken breast halves (about 1½ lbs.** *total***)**

Heat oil in a 10- to 12-inch frying pan over medium heat. Add shallots and mushrooms; cook, stirring occasionally, until shallots are soft (about 5 minutes). Add broccoli and Madeira, cover and cook, stirring occasionally, until broccoli is tender-crisp to bite (about 5 minutes). Remove from heat and stir in Parmesan cheese and ¼ cup of the Swiss cheese. Let cool.

Rinse chicken and pat dry. Place each breast half between 2 sheets of plastic wrap; pound with a flat-surfaced mallet to a thickness of about ¼ inch.

In center of each breast half, mound a sixth of the broccoli mixture. Roll chicken around filling to enclose. Set rolls, seam side down, in a greased 9- by 13-inch baking pan. Sprinkle with remaining ¼ cup Swiss cheese.

Bake, uncovered, in a 450° oven until meat is no longer pink and filling is hot in center; cut to test (about 15 minutes). Then broil chicken 4 to 6 inches below heat until cheese is golden brown (about 2 minutes). Makes 6 servings.

Per serving: 232 calories, 33 g protein, 9 g carbohydrates, 7 g fat, 3 g saturated fat, 76 mg cholesterol, 145 mg sodium

CHICKEN BREASTS WITH FETA CHEESE

Preparation time: About 15 minutes

Cooking time: About 10 minutes

Fresh lemon juice and salty feta cheese give sautéed chicken a distinctive tang. Add a simple rice pilaf and steamed tiny artichokes for a satisfying Mediterranean meal.

- 8 **ounces feta cheese, crumbled**
- ¼ **cup chopped fresh oregano leaves**
- 6 **skinless, boneless chicken breast halves (about 1½ lbs.** *total***)**
- 1 **tablespoon butter or margarine**
- 1 **tablespoon salad oil**
  Juice of 1 lemon

In a small bowl, combine cheese and oregano; set aside.

Rinse chicken and pat dry. Place each breast half between 2 sheets of plastic wrap; pound with a flat-surfaced mallet to a thickness of about ¼ inch. In center of each breast half, mound a sixth of the cheese mixture. Fold chicken over filling to enclose.

Melt butter in oil in a 12- to 14-inch frying pan over medium-high heat. Add chicken and lemon juice. Cook, turning as needed, until meat is golden brown on both sides and no longer pink in center, and cheese filling is hot; cut to test (about 10 minutes). Makes 6 servings.

Per serving: 265 calories, 32 g protein, 2 g carbohydrates, 14 g fat, 8 g saturated fat, 105 mg cholesterol, 515 mg sodium

Flavorful Chicken in Port Cream with Fettuccine (recipe on facing page) deserves to be shown off at your next party—perhaps with a side dish of steamed asparagus. Chopped dried tomatoes and a cup of wine give the sauce its rich, rosy color.

CHICKEN BREASTS WITH PARMESAN PESTO

Preparation time: About 20 minutes

Cooking time: About 10 minutes

Pesto is usually tossed with pasta, but that doesn't mean you can't use it in other ways too. Here, we enclose the basil-rich sauce in pounded chicken breasts. Garnish the dish with blooming basil sprigs from your garden or a produce market.

> 6 **skinless, boneless chicken breast halves (about 1½ lbs. *total*)**
> 1 **cup lightly packed fresh basil leaves**
> ¾ **cup grated Parmesan cheese**
> ¼ **cup olive oil**
> 1 **small clove garlic**
> 1½ **tablespoons butter or margarine**
> 1½ **tablespoons olive oil**
> **About ⅓ cup all-purpose flour**
> **Basil sprigs**

Rinse chicken and pat dry. Place each breast half between 2 sheets of plastic wrap; pound with a flat-surfaced mallet to a thickness of about ¼ inch. Set aside.

In a blender or food processor, combine basil leaves, cheese, the ¼ cup oil, and garlic; whirl to form a thick paste. Then mound a sixth of the pesto in center of each pounded chicken breast half; roll chicken around pesto to enclose.

Melt butter in the 1½ tablespoons oil in a 12- to 14-inch frying pan over medium-high heat. Dip each chicken roll in flour and shake off excess; add chicken to pan. Cook, turning as needed, until meat is golden brown on all sides and no longer pink in center, and filling is hot; cut to test (about 10 minutes). Transfer to a serving dish and garnish with basil sprigs. Makes 6 servings.

Per serving: 338 calories, 32 g protein, 8 g carbohydrates, 20 g fat, 6 g saturated fat, 81 mg cholesterol, 290 mg sodium

Pictured on facing page

CHICKEN IN PORT CREAM WITH FETTUCCINE

Preparation time: About 5 minutes, plus about 1 hour to soak tomatoes

Cooking time: About 20 minutes

Pasta couldn't be better served than by sautéed chicken in a port-infused cream sauce flecked with chunks of dried tomatoes. Offer plenty of crisp-crusted bread to soak up the extra sauce.

> ¾ **cup dried tomatoes**
> 6 **skinless, boneless chicken breast halves (about 1½ lbs. *total*)**
> 3 **tablespoons butter or margarine**
> 1 **cup port**
> 1½ **cups whipping cream**
> 1 **package (9 oz.) fresh fettuccine or 8 ounces dry fettuccine**
> **Salt and pepper**
> **Tarragon sprigs**

In a small bowl, soak tomatoes in warm water to cover until soft (about 1 hour). Drain well, chop coarsely, and set aside.

Rinse chicken and pat dry. Melt butter in a 12- to 14-inch frying pan over medium-high heat. Add chicken and cook, turning as needed, until well browned on both sides and no longer pink in center; cut to test (about 10 minutes). Remove from pan and keep warm.

To pan drippings, add port and cream. Increase heat to high and bring mixture to a boil; boil, stirring occasionally, until large, shiny bubbles form (about 10 minutes). Meanwhile, cook fettuccine according to package directions just until tender to bite. Drain well; transfer to a deep platter and keep warm.

Add tomatoes to cream mixture; then add chicken and any accumulated juices. Season to taste with salt and pepper. Spoon chicken and sauce over fettuccine; garnish with tarragon sprigs. Makes 6 servings.

Per serving: 519 calories, 34 g protein, 36 g carbohydrates, 27 g fat, 16 g saturated fat, 198 mg cholesterol, 179 mg sodium

MINI-HEN MEALS

Cornish game hens can truly be called mini-chickens. Developed from the Cornish breed of chicken, these little birds weigh in at just 1¼ to 1½ pounds—the perfect size for one or two servings. And because their meat is so mild in flavor, game hens are compatible with all sorts of seasonings, sauces, and marinades.

For an elegant evening, try butterflied hens brushed with a mustard coating and roasted with rosemary; if you're planning a romantic dinner for two, simmer a single bird in red wine sauce with carrots, onions, and spinach. Family and guests alike will enjoy roasted birds with an unusual vegetable "hash" featuring yams and jicama. Grilled hens with a flavorful balsamic marinade are another sure success.

Pictured on page 127

GAME HENS WITH MUSTARD CRUST

Preparation time: About 15 minutes

Roasting time: About 25 minutes

   ¼ **cup butter or margarine, melted**
   ¼ **cup Dijon mustard**
   1 **tablespoon minced fresh rosemary; or 1 tablespoon dry rosemary, crumbled**
   2 **cloves garlic, minced or pressed**
   4 **Cornish game hens (1¼ to 1½ lbs. *each*), thawed if frozen**
      Rosemary sprigs (optional)
      Salt and pepper

In a small bowl, stir together butter, mustard, minced rosemary, and garlic. Set aside.

Reserve game hen necks and giblets for other uses. With poultry shears or a knife, split hens lengthwise along one side of backbone. Pull hens open; place, skin side up, on a flat surface and press firmly, cracking bones slightly, until hens lie reasonably flat. Rinse hens and pat dry. Coat both sides of each hen with mustard mixture; then set hens, skin side up, slightly apart in 2 shallow 10- by 15-inch baking pans.

Roast, uncovered, in a 350° oven, switching positions of pans halfway through baking, until meat near thighbone is no longer pink; cut to test (about 25 minutes). Transfer hens to a platter or dinner plates. Garnish with rosemary sprigs, if desired; season to taste with salt and pepper. Makes 4 servings.

Per serving: 783 calories, 75 g protein, 3 g carbohydrates, 50 g fat, 18 g saturated fat, 274 mg cholesterol, 794 mg sodium

GAME HEN DINNER FOR TWO

Preparation time: About 15 minutes

Cooking time: About 35 minutes

   1 **Cornish game hen (about 1½ lbs.), thawed if frozen**
   2 **tablespoons butter or margarine**
   6 **small onions (*each* about 1 inch in diameter), peeled**
   1 **cup regular-strength beef broth**
   ½ **cup dry red wine**
   1 **tablespoon Dijon mustard**
   ½ **teaspoon dry basil leaves**
   3 **slender carrots, cut in half crosswise**
   8 **ounces spinach**

Reserve game hen neck and giblets for other uses. With poultry shears or a knife, split hen in half, cutting lengthwise through breastbone and along one side of backbone. Rinse hen and pat dry.

Melt butter in a 12- to 14-inch frying pan over medium heat. Add game hen halves and onions; cook, turning as needed, until well browned on all sides (about 15 minutes). Remove hen halves and onions from pan; set aside.

Add broth to pan and boil over high heat, stirring to scrape up browned bits, until reduced to ⅓ cup. Blend in wine, mustard, and basil.

Return hen halves and onions to pan; add carrots. Reduce heat, cover, and simmer until meat near thighbone is no longer pink; cut to test (about 15 minutes). Meanwhile, discard stems and any wilted leaves from spinach; wash and drain remaining leaves.

Mound hen halves, onions, and carrots to one side of pan. Push spinach into broth and stir until wilted. Serve hen halves and vegetables with broth. Makes 2 servings.

Per serving: 700 calories, 48 g protein, 19 g carbohydrates, 48 g fat, 17 g saturated fat, 205 mg cholesterol, 1,023 mg sodium

ROAST GAME HENS WITH VEGETABLE HASH

Preparation time: About 20 minutes

Roasting time: About 1 hour

2 **Cornish game hens (1¼ to 1½ lbs.** *each***), thawed if frozen**

3 **tablespoons lemon juice**

3 **tablespoons olive oil or salad oil**

2 **teaspoons minced fresh rosemary; or 2 teaspoons dry rosemary, crumbled**

1 **clove garlic, minced or pressed**

1 **small jicama (about 1 lb.), peeled and cut into ½-inch cubes**

2 **large yams or sweet potatoes (about 1 lb.** *total***), scrubbed and cut into ½-inch cubes**

1 **large red or yellow bell pepper (about 6 oz.), seeded and diced**

1 **large onion, coarsely chopped**

1 **package (10 oz.) frozen baby lima beans, thawed**

   Salt and pepper

   Rosemary sprigs

Reserve game hen necks and giblets for other uses. With poultry shears or a knife, split hens lengthwise through breastbone and along one side of backbone. Rinse hens and pat dry.

In an 12- by 17-inch roasting pan, mix lemon juice, oil, minced rosemary, and garlic. Turn hen halves in oil mixture to coat; lift out and set aside. Add jicama, yams, bell pepper, and onion to pan; stir to coat.

Roast vegetables, uncovered, in a 425° oven for 30 minutes. Stir in beans. Lay hen halves, skin side up, on vegetables and continue to roast, uncovered, until meat near thighbone is no longer pink; cut to test (about 30 more minutes).

Transfer hen halves to a large platter; spoon vegetables alongside. Season to taste with salt and pepper. Garnish with rosemary sprigs. Makes 4 servings.

Per serving: 664 calories, 35 g protein, 60 g carbohydrates, 32 g fat, 7 g saturated fat, 103 mg cholesterol, 153 mg sodium

GRILLED GAME HENS

Preparation time: About 20 minutes

Marinating time: At least 1 hour or up to 1 day

Grilling time: About 30 minutes

   Balsamic Marinade (recipe follows)

4 **Cornish game hens (about 1¼ lbs.** *each***), thawed if frozen**

2 **medium-size zucchini (about 12 oz.** *total***), cut diagonally into ½-inch-thick slices**

2 **medium-size crookneck squash (about 8 oz.** *total***), cut diagonally into ½-inch-thick slices**

1 **large red bell pepper (about 6 oz.), seeded and cut into 1½-inch squares**

8 **large mushrooms, stems trimmed**

8 **large shallots (about 8 oz.** *total***), peeled**

   Salt

Prepare Balsamic Marinade; set aside.

Reserve game hen necks and giblets for other uses. With poultry shears or a knife, split hens lengthwise through breastbone. Pull hens open; place, skin side up, on a flat surface and press firmly, cracking bones slightly, until hens lie reasonably flat.

Place hens in a large heavy-duty plastic bag. Place zucchini, crookneck squash, bell pepper, mushrooms, and shallots in a second heavy-duty plastic bag. Pour half the marinade into each bag; seal bags and turn over several times to coat hens and vegetables with marinade. Set bags in a large, shallow baking pan or dish. Refrigerate for at least 1 hour or up to 1 day, turning bags over occasionally.

Drain hens and vegetables; reserve marinade. Using a pair of parallel metal skewers (at least 12 to 15 inches long), thread 2 hens from wing to wing and from thigh to thigh to hold them flat. Repeat to skewer remaining 2 hens, using another pair of skewers. Then thread each kind of vegetable separately on 5 additional 12- to 15-inch metal skewers.

Place birds (skin side up) and vegetables on a lightly greased grill 4 to 6 inches above a solid bed of medium coals. Cook, turning often and basting with marinade, until meat near thighbone is no longer pink; cut to test (about 30 minutes).

To serve, push foods off skewers. Season to taste with salt. Makes 4 servings.

BALSAMIC MARINADE. In a bowl, stir together ⅔ cup **balsamic vinegar** or red wine vinegar, 4 teaspoons **Dijon mustard**, 2 teaspoons minced **parsley**, 2 teaspoons minced **fresh thyme leaves** or about ¾ teaspoon dry thyme leaves, and ⅛ teaspoon **pepper**.

Per serving: 685 calories, 73 g protein, 19 g carbohydrates, 35 g fat, 10 g saturated fat, 220 mg cholesterol, 292 mg sodium

CALIFORNIA CHICKEN SEAFOOD

Preparation time: About 15 minutes

Cooking time: About 30 minutes

Does the chicken complement the seafood—or are the scallops and shrimp added to enhance the chicken? One thing's for sure: the cognac-laced cream sauce tastes wonderful with everything.

> 8 **ounces medium-size raw shrimp (about 48 per lb.)**
>
> **Shrimp Stock (recipe follows)**
>
> 2 **tablespoons butter or margarine**
>
> 1 **tablespoon salad oil**
>
> 6 **skinless, boneless chicken breast halves (about 1½ lbs. *total*)**
>
> 4 **ounces scallops, rinsed well and drained**
>
> ¾ **cup whipping cream**
>
> ¼ **cup cognac or brandy**
>
> **Whole chives**
>
> **Salt and pepper**

Shell and devein shrimp, reserving shells for Shrimp Stock. Cover and refrigerate shrimp; prepare Shrimp Stock.

Melt butter in oil in a 12- to 14-inch frying pan over medium-high heat. Add chicken and cook, turning as needed, until well browned on both sides and no longer pink in center; cut to test (about 10 minutes). Remove chicken from pan and keep warm.

If using sea scallops, cut them into ½-inch chunks. Add scallops and shrimp to pan. Cook, stirring often, until shrimp are opaque throughout; cut to test (about 3 minutes). Remove from pan; set aside. Add Shrimp Stock, cream, and cognac to pan and boil over high heat, stirring frequently, until sauce is reduced to about ¾ cup and large, shiny bubbles form (about 5 minutes).

Reduce heat to medium. Return chicken and any accumulated juices, shrimp, and scallops to pan. Turn to coat with sauce. Arrange in a serving dish and garnish with chives; season to taste with salt and pepper. Makes 6 servings.

SHRIMP STOCK. In a 2- to 3-quart pan, combine **reserved shrimp shells** and 1 cup *each* **dry white wine** and **regular-strength chicken broth.** Bring to a boil over high heat; boil, uncovered, until liquid is reduced by half. Pour through a fine strainer; discard shells. Return stock to pan and boil until reduced to about ½ cup.

Per serving: 321 calories, 37 g protein, 2 g carbohydrates, 18 g fat, 9 g saturated fat, 162 mg cholesterol, 365 mg sodium

DOUBLE CHEESE CHICKEN BREASTS

Preparation time: About 15 minutes

Cooking time: About 4 minutes

Chicken is treated to cheese times two—first coated with a Parmesan crust, then covered with melted mozzarella. Choose colorful accompaniments for this quick-to-cook dish; sliced tomatoes and steamed zucchini are good selections.

> 4 **skinless, boneless chicken breast halves (about 1 lb. *total*)**
>
> 4 **slices white bread, torn into pieces**
>
> ¼ **cup *each* chopped parsley and grated Parmesan cheese**
>
> **About ¼ teaspoon *each* salt and pepper**
>
> 1 **large egg, lightly beaten**
>
> **About 2 tablespoons salad oil**
>
> ½ **cup shredded mozzarella cheese**

Rinse chicken and pat dry. Place each breast half between 2 sheets of plastic wrap; pound with a flat-surfaced mallet to a thickness of about ¼ inch. Set aside.

Place bread in a blender or food processor and whirl to form coarse crumbs. In a wide, shallow rimmed plate, combine crumbs, parsley, Parmesan cheese, salt, and pepper. Dip each pounded chicken breast half in egg; then press into crumb mixture to coat well.

Heat 2 tablespoons of the oil in a 12- to 14-inch frying pan over medium-high heat. Add chicken and cook, turning as needed, until golden on both sides (about 3 minutes); add a little more oil, if necessary. Sprinkle each piece with 2 tablespoons of the mozzarella cheese; cover pan and continue to cook just until cheese is melted. Makes 4 servings.

Per serving: 333 calories, 35 g protein, 13 g carbohydrates, 15 g fat, 5 g saturated fat, 135 mg cholesterol, 494 mg sodium

When scallops and shrimp combine with chicken, the result is a
culinary success story: California Chicken Seafood (recipe on facing page).
Credit a creamy-rich, cognac-infused sauce for this meal's winning flavor.
Accompany with warm sourdough bread and steamed green beans
topped with toasted almonds.

PASTA & CHICKEN IN SWEET-SOUR TOMATO SAUCE

Preparation time: About 10 minutes

Cooking time: About 25 minutes

Sautéed chicken strips surround a bed of linguine for this elegant, easy main dish. Family and friends may not be able to guess what goes into the rich tomato sauce, but they're sure to enjoy the contrasting flavors.

- 3 **tablespoons olive oil**
- 1 **medium-size onion, thinly sliced**
- 2 **tablespoons pine nuts or slivered blanched almonds**
- 2 **cloves garlic, minced or pressed**
- 6 **medium-size pear-shaped tomatoes (about 12 oz. *total*), chopped**
- 1 **tablespoon *each* firmly packed brown sugar and dried currants**
- 2 **tablespoons cider vinegar**
- ½ **teaspoon ground allspice**
- ¾ **cup dry red wine**
- 4 **skinless, boneless chicken breast halves (about 1 lb. *total*)**
- 8 **ounces dry linguine or 1 package (9 oz.) fresh linguine**
  Salt and pepper
  Chopped parsley

Heat 2 tablespoons of the oil in a 10- to 12-inch frying pan over medium heat. Add onion and pine nuts and cook, stirring, until onion is soft (about 10 minutes). Stir in garlic, tomatoes, sugar, currants, vinegar, allspice, and wine. Adjust heat so mixture boils gently. Continue to cook, uncovered, stirring occasionally, until sauce is slightly thickened (about 15 minutes).

Meanwhile, rinse chicken and pat dry. Brush on all sides with remaining 1 tablespoon oil. Place a ridged cooktop grill pan over medium heat; heat until a drop of water dances on the surface. Place chicken on hot pan and cook, turning as needed, until well browned on both sides and no longer pink in center; cut to test (about 10 minutes).

While chicken is cooking, cook linguine according to package directions just until tender to bite. Drain well.

Season tomato sauce to taste with salt and pepper. Add linguine and mix lightly, using 2 forks. Transfer to a deep platter. Cut chicken across the grain into ½-inch-wide strips; arrange around edge of linguine. Sprinkle with parsley. Makes 4 servings.

Per serving: 497 calories, 36 g protein, 55 g carbohydrates, 15 g fat, 2 g saturated fat, 66 mg cholesterol, 89 mg sodium

CHICKEN BREASTS WITH BLUEBERRIES

Preparation time: About 5 minutes

Cooking time: About 21 minutes

Just half a cup of blueberries makes a definite contribution to the taste—and the color—of this dish. The sauce features apricot jam to enhance the berries' sweetness; mustard and wine vinegar add tang.

- 4 **skinless, boneless chicken breast halves (about 1 lb. *total*)**
- 1 **tablespoon salad oil**
- ½ **cup apricot jam**
- 3 **tablespoons Dijon mustard**
- ½ **cup frozen unsweetened blueberries**
- ⅓ **cup white wine vinegar**
  Watercress sprigs

Rinse chicken and pat dry. Heat oil in a 10- to 12-inch frying pan over medium-high heat. Add chicken; cook, turning as needed, until lightly browned on both sides (about 6 minutes).

Meanwhile, in a small bowl, stir together jam and mustard. Spread jam mixture over browned chicken; sprinkle with blueberries. Reduce heat to low, cover, and cook until meat in thickest part is no longer pink; cut to test (about 10 minutes; turn chicken over after 5 minutes). With a slotted spoon, lift chicken and blueberries to a platter; keep warm.

Add vinegar to pan, increase heat to high, and bring to a boil. Boil, stirring occasionally, until sauce is thickened (about 5 minutes). Pour sauce over chicken; garnish with watercress. Makes 4 servings.

Per serving: 290 calories, 27 g protein, 33 g carbohydrates, 6 g fat, 1 g saturated fat, 66 mg cholesterol, 416 mg sodium

SPICED CHICKEN WITH CAPERS

Preparation time: About 10 minutes

Cooking time: About 22 minutes

The old adage "opposites attract" may not always hold true—but the contrasting flavors of this dish will certainly bring your guests back for more. The sweetness of cinnamon, cloves, and raisins beautifully complements the tartness of capers and orange juice. Serve over rice, if you like.

  4 **skinless, boneless chicken breast halves (about 1 lb. *total*)**
  2 **tablespoons salad oil**
  1 **large onion, thinly sliced**
  2 **cloves garlic, minced or pressed**
  ¼ **teaspoon *each* ground cinnamon and ground cloves**
  ½ **cup orange juice**
  2 **tablespoons raisins**
  1 **tablespoon drained capers**
      Parsley sprigs (optional)
      Salt and pepper

Rinse chicken and pat dry. Heat oil in a 10- to 12-inch frying pan over medium-high heat. Add chicken and cook, turning as needed, until lightly browned on both sides (about 6 minutes). Remove from pan and set aside.

Add onion and garlic to pan; cook, stirring often, until onion is lightly browned (about 6 minutes). Stir in cinnamon, cloves, orange juice, raisins, and capers. Return chicken and any accumulated juices to pan. Reduce heat to low, cover, and simmer until meat in thickest part is no longer pink; cut to test (about 10 minutes; turn chicken over after 5 minutes).

Transfer chicken and sauce to a serving dish and garnish with parsley, if desired. Season to taste with salt and pepper. Makes 4 servings.

Per serving: 229 calories, 27 g protein, 11 g carbohydrates, 8 g fat, 1 g saturated fat, 66 mg cholesterol, 131 mg sodium

CREAMY CHICKEN ROULADES

Preparation time: About 20 minutes

Cooking time: About 15 minutes

Looking for "company's coming" chicken? These cheese-filled rolls in sour cream–white wine sauce will be welcomed by the most discriminating diner.

  4 **skinless, boneless chicken breast halves (about 1 lb. *total*)**
  ½ **cup shredded mozzarella cheese**
  3 **tablespoons butter or margarine**
  1 **clove garlic, minced or pressed**
  2 **teaspoons chopped parsley**
  3 **tablespoons dry white wine**
  ¼ **cup all-purpose flour**
  ¼ **teaspoon *each* paprika and pepper**
  ½ **cup regular-strength chicken broth**
  ½ **cup sour cream**
      Salt

Rinse chicken and pat dry. Place each breast half between 2 sheets of plastic wrap; pound with a flat-surfaced mallet to a thickness of about ¼ inch. Top each piece of chicken with 2 tablespoons of the

cheese, 1 teaspoon of the butter, a fourth of the garlic, ½ teaspoon of the parsley, and 1 teaspoon of the wine. Roll chicken around filling to enclose, securing rolls with wooden picks.

In a paper or plastic bag, combine flour, paprika, and pepper. Shake chicken pieces in bag to coat evenly with flour mixture; shake off excess. Reserve remaining flour mixture.

Melt remaining butter in a 10- to 12-inch frying pan over medium heat. Add chicken and cook, turning as needed, until lightly browned on all sides (about 6 minutes). Add broth. Reduce heat, cover, and simmer until meat is no longer pink and filling is hot; cut to test (about 6 minutes). With a slotted spoon, transfer chicken to a platter; remove wooden picks.

Blend remaining wine with 1 teaspoon of the reserved flour mixture; stir wine mixture into sour cream, then whisk mixture into pan juices. Cook over high heat, stirring, until sauce just comes to a boil. Pour sauce over chicken. Season to taste with salt. Makes 4 servings.

Per serving: 337 calories, 31 g protein, 8 g carbohydrates, 19 g fat, 11 g saturated fat, 113 mg cholesterol, 354 mg sodium

Guests will never guess this entrée is a diet-conscious diner's delight—but saucy Apricot–Dijon Mustard Chicken (recipe on facing page) served over the "super grain" quinoa is both low in fat and high in protein. Complete the menu with dinner rolls and a salad of butter lettuce, mandarin oranges, red onions, walnuts, and watercress in vinaigrette.

STUFFED CHICKEN BREASTS WITH CHUTNEY

Preparation time: About 35 minutes

Cooking time: About 15 minutes

Here's a low-fat meal elegant enough for a party. Tender chicken is wrapped around a stuffing of fresh spinach, sautéed garlic, and onions, then simmered in a tangy chutney sauce.

- 1 tablespoon olive oil
- 2 cloves garlic, minced or pressed
- 1 large onion, chopped
- 2¼ cups chopped spinach leaves
- 8 skinless, boneless chicken breast halves (about 2 lbs. *total*)
- 1 tablespoon balsamic vinegar
- ½ cup low-sodium chicken broth
- ¼ cup chopped chutney

Heat oil in a 12- to 14-inch frying pan over medium-high heat. Add garlic and onion and cook, stirring occasionally, until onion is soft (about 7 minutes).

Add 2 cups of the spinach; remove from heat and let cool.

Rinse chicken and pat dry. Place each breast half between 2 sheets of plastic wrap; pound with a flat-surfaced mallet to a thickness of about ¼ inch. In center of each breast half, mound an eighth of the spinach mixture; roll chicken around filling to enclose. Place chicken rolls in pan used for spinach mixture.

In a small bowl, mix vinegar, broth, and chutney. Pour over chicken. Bring to a simmer over medium heat. Cover and simmer until meat is no longer pink and filling is hot; cut to test (about 8 minutes). With a slotted spoon, lift chicken from pan and place on a platter; keep warm.

Boil pan juices over high heat, stirring occasionally, until reduced to ½ cup (about 5 minutes); then pour over chicken. Garnish with remaining ¼ cup spinach. Makes 8 servings.

Per serving: 174 calories, 27 g protein, 8 g carbohydrates, 3 g fat, 1g saturated fat, 66 mg cholesterol, 107 mg sodium

■ *Pictured on facing page*

APRICOT–DIJON MUSTARD CHICKEN

Preparation time: About 5 minutes

Cooking time: About 25 minutes

Creating a meal that's wholesome *and* irresistibly appetizing can be a challenge. This flavorful dish fills the bill: boneless chicken breasts are simmered in apricot nectar and Dijon mustard, then served on seasoned quinoa. (You'll find this high-protein grain in health food stores and well-stocked supermarkets.)

- 6 skinless, boneless chicken breast halves (about 1½ lbs. *total*)
- 1 can (12 oz.) apricot nectar
- 3 tablespoons Dijon mustard
- 3 cups regular-strength chicken broth
- 1½ cups quinoa
- 2 tablespoons minced fresh basil leaves
  Basil sprigs
  Lime halves and wedges

Rinse chicken and pat dry; set aside.

In a 12- to 14-inch frying pan, combine apricot nectar and mustard; bring to a boil over high heat. Then place chicken breasts, skinned side down, in pan. Reduce heat to medium-low, cover, and simmer until meat in thickest part is no longer pink; cut to test (about 15 minutes; turn chicken pieces over after 10 minutes).

Meanwhile, in a 2- to 3-quart pan, bring broth to a boil over high heat. Stir in quinoa; reduce heat, cover, and simmer until grain is tender and liquid is absorbed (about 15 minutes).

Fluff quinoa with a fork; pour onto a platter. With a slotted spoon, lift chicken from pan and place atop quinoa; cover and keep warm. Boil pan juices over high heat, partially covered, until reduced to 1 cup (about 5 minutes); then pour over chicken. Sprinkle with minced basil; garnish with basil sprigs and lime halves. Accompany with lime wedges to squeeze over meat. Makes 6 servings.

Per serving: 344 calories, 34 g protein, 40 g carbohydrates, 5 g fat, 1 g saturated fat, 66 mg cholesterol, 820 mg sodium

CHICKEN ON COOL GREENS

Preparation time: About 15 minutes

Marinating time: At least 30 minutes or up to 1 day

Cooking time: About 15 minutes

A generous helping of minced shallots goes into a mustardy vinaigrette that doubles as a marinade for chicken and a dressing for your choice of greens. Just broil the marinated boneless breasts, cut them into strips, and serve warm over a crisp salad.

  4   **boneless chicken breast halves (about 1¼ lbs. *total*)**
  ⅓   **cup salad oil or olive oil**
  3   **tablespoons white wine vinegar**
  1   **tablespoon Dijon mustard**
  1   **clove garlic, minced or pressed**
  ¼   **cup minced shallots**
  8   **to 10 cups bite-size pieces washed, crisped mixed salad greens, such as chicory, leaf lettuce, arugula, butter lettuce, and escarole**
      Salt and pepper

Rinse chicken and pat dry. Set aside.

In a small bowl, prepare dressing by mixing oil, vinegar, mustard, garlic, and shallots. Place chicken in a large bowl and pour ¼ cup of the dressing over it; turn chicken to coat. Cover and refrigerate for at least 30 minutes or up to 1 day. Also cover and refrigerate remaining dressing.

Drain chicken; discard marinade. Place chicken, skin side up, on rack of a 10- by 15-inch broiling pan. Broil about 4 inches below heat, turning as needed to brown evenly, until meat in thickest part is no longer pink; cut to test (about 15 minutes).

Shortly before chicken is done, mix greens with remaining dressing. Divide salad equally among 4 dinner plates. Cut each chicken breast half across the grain into ½-inch-wide strips; arrange one sliced half atop each serving of salad. Season to taste with salt and pepper. Makes 4 servings.

Per serving: 338 calories, 30 g protein, 4 g carbohydrates, 22 g fat, 4 g saturated fat, 81 mg cholesterol, 171 mg sodium

CHINESE NOODLE SALAD WITH FIVE-SPICE CHICKEN

Preparation time: About 15 minutes

Grilling time: About 15 minutes

Warm barbecued chicken breasts and cool pasta rest side by side on a bed of crisp spinach leaves. The Asian-accented dressing features rice vinegar, sesame oil, and fragrant five-spice.

      Five-spice Dressing (recipe follows)
  10 **ounces (3 cups; part of a 14-oz. package) fresh Chinese-style noodles**
  ½   **cup chopped fresh cilantro (coriander)**
  1   **tablespoon grated fresh ginger**
  ½   **teaspoon grated lemon peel**
  4   **skinless, boneless chicken breast halves (about 1 lb. *total*)**
  4   **to 6 cups spinach leaves, washed and crisped**
  ¼   **cup thinly sliced green onions (including tops)**

Prepare Five-spice Dressing; set aside.

In a 5- to 6-quart pan, cook noodles in 3 quarts boiling water just until tender to bite (about 2 minutes). Drain, immerse in cold water until cool, drain again, and place in a large bowl. Add ⅓ cup of the dressing; then gently mix in cilantro, ginger, and lemon peel. Set aside.

Rinse chicken and pat dry. Place on a lightly greased grill 4 to 6 inches above a solid bed of medium-hot coals. Cook, turning once and basting several times with the remaining dressing, until meat in thickest part is no longer pink; cut to test (about 15 minutes). Remove chicken to a board and cut across the grain into ½-inch-wide strips.

Line 4 dinner plates with spinach. Top equally with warm chicken and noodles, arranging separately. Sprinkle with onions. Makes 4 servings.

FIVE-SPICE DRESSING. In a small bowl, combine 2 tablespoons **seasoned rice vinegar** (or 2 tablespoons rice vinegar and 1 teaspoon sugar); 1 tablespoon *each* **soy sauce, Oriental sesame oil,** and **lemon juice;** 1 clove **garlic,** minced or pressed; ½ teaspoon **Chinese five-spice** (or ¼ teaspoon *each* anise seeds and ground ginger and ⅛ teaspoon *each* ground cinnamon and ground cloves); and ¼ cup **salad oil.**

Per serving: 510 calories, 33 g protein, 44 g carbohydrates, 20 g fat, 3g saturated fat, 149 mg cholesterol, 409 mg sodium

SMOKED CHICKEN SALAD WITH MANGO DRESSING

Preparation time: About 15 minutes, plus 30 minutes to heat coals and 20 minutes to soak wood chips

Marinating time: At least 4 hours or up to 1 day

Grilling time: About 20 minutes

Greet guests with fruity flavor and fragrance when you prepare this very special salad.

- 1 tablespoon *each* chopped fresh ginger and grated orange peel
- ⅓ cup *each* soy sauce, orange juice, and oyster sauce
- 8 skinless, boneless chicken breast halves (about 2 lbs. *total*)

  Mango Dressing (recipe follows)

  About 1 cup fruit wood chips, such as cherry or apple, soaked in water for 20 minutes and drained
- 4 quarts bite-size pieces washed, crisped mixed salad greens, such as watercress, leaf lettuce, and butter lettuce
- 1 *each* medium-size red and yellow bell pepper, seeded and thinly sliced

In a large bowl, combine ginger, orange peel, soy, orange juice, and oyster sauce. Rinse chicken and pat dry; add to marinade and turn to coat. Cover and refrigerate for at least 4 hours or up to 1 day, turning several times.

Prepare Mango Dressing and set aside.

Prepare a covered barbecue for grilling by indirect heat as directed for Barbecued Turkey on page 22. After banking coals, sprinkle each pile of coals with half the wet wood chips. Set cooking grill in place 4 to 6 inches above drip pan; lightly grease grill.

Drain chicken; place on grill directly above drip pan. Cover barbecue; adjust dampers as necessary to maintain an even heat. Cook chicken until meat in thickest part is no longer pink; cut to test (about 20 minutes). Cut across the grain into ½-inch-wide strips.

To serve, divide greens among 8 dinner plates. Arrange chicken and bell peppers over greens. Offer Mango Dressing to add to taste. Makes 8 servings.

Per serving without dressing: 150 calories, 28 g protein, 4 g carbohydrates, 2 g fat, 0 g saturated fat, 66 mg cholesterol, 378 mg sodium

MANGO DRESSING. Peel 2 ripe **mangoes** (about 1½ lbs. *total*). Slice fruit from pits; discard pits. Place fruit in a blender or food processor; add ⅓ cup **orange juice** and 2 tablespoons *each* **Oriental sesame oil** and **balsamic vinegar.** Whirl until smooth. Makes 2 cups.

Per tablespoon: 18 calories, 0 g protein, 3 g carbohydrates, 1 g fat, 0 g saturated fat, 0 mg cholesterol, 0 mg sodium

CHICKEN PICADILLO

Preparation time: About 45 minutes

Baking time: About 1½ hours

Hearty, piquant, colorful, and low in fat, this stew would be hard to improve!

- 1 tablespoon olive oil
- 1½ pounds skinless, boneless chicken breasts, cut into 1½-inch chunks
- 1 large onion, chopped
- 2 cloves garlic, minced or pressed
- 1 medium-size green bell pepper, seeded and chopped
- 1 large can (15 oz.) no-salt-added tomato sauce
- 1 cup dry white wine
- 1 fresh jalapeño chile, thinly sliced, seeded
- 1½ teaspoons dry oregano leaves
- 1 teaspoon dry thyme leaves
- 1½ pounds small red thin-skinned potatoes (*each* 1½ to 2 inches in diameter)
- ½ cup pimento-stuffed olives, thinly sliced
- ½ cup raisins
- 1 cup frozen peas, thawed
- ¼ cup slivered blanched almonds

Heat oil in a 12- to 14-inch frying pan over medium heat. Add chicken and cook, stirring often, until browned on all sides (about 6 minutes). Transfer chicken to a 4- to 5-quart casserole.

Add onion, garlic, and bell pepper to pan; cook, stirring occasionally, until onion is soft (about 10 minutes). Add tomato sauce, wine, chile, oregano, and thyme; cook, stirring occasionally, until sauce comes to a boil. Boil gently, uncovered, for 5 minutes. Scrub and quarter unpeeled potatoes.

Pour sauce over chicken; add potatoes, olives, and raisins. Cover and bake in a 375° oven until potatoes are tender when pierced (about 1½ hours). Stir in peas and almonds. Makes 6 servings.

Per serving: 380 calories, 33 g protein, 44 g carbohydrates, 9 g fat, 1 g saturated fat, 66 mg cholesterol, 402 mg sodium

SAKE-STEAMED CHICKEN BREASTS WITH RICE

Preparation time: About 10 minutes

Marinating time: At least 30 minutes or up to 2 hours

Cooking time: About 12 minutes

You can use a fork, chopsticks, or just your fingers for this light meal. Dip each bite of meat in horseradish-spiked soy sauce before eating.

6 **skinless, boneless chicken breast halves (about 1½ lbs.** *total***)**

½ **cup sake or rice vinegar**

½ **teaspoon salt**

1 **small head iceberg lettuce (about 1¼ lbs.), separated into leaves, washed, and crisped**

About ¼ cup soy sauce

About 1 tablespoon prepared horseradish

Hot cooked rice

Slivered green onions (including tops) or black sesame seeds

Lemon wedges

Rinse chicken and pat dry. In a bowl, stir together sake and salt until salt is dissolved. Add chicken; turn to coat, then cover and refrigerate for at least 30 minutes or up to 2 hours. Drain chicken; discard marinade. Arrange chicken in a single layer in a 10- or 11-inch glass pie dish or rimmed plate. Cover dish with wax paper or foil; set dish on a rack in a large pan above 1 to 2 inches of boiling water. Cover and steam until meat in thickest part is no longer pink; cut to test (about 12 minutes).

While chicken is cooking, place 1 or 2 large lettuce leaves on each of 6 dinner plates. Finely cut remaining lettuce into long, thin shreds; pile equally onto whole leaves. Also, for each plate, pour about 2 teaspoons of the soy into a tiny bowl and add about ½ teaspoon of the horseradish; set bowl on plate.

Cut chicken across the grain into ½-inch-wide strips. Spoon rice alongside lettuce and divide chicken among plates; sprinkle with onions or sesame seeds and garnish with lemon wedges.

To eat, squeeze lemon into soy-horseradish sauce; dip chicken into sauce and eat with rice and shredded lettuce. Or tear lettuce leaves into large portions and wrap up bits of sauce-dipped chicken, rice, and shredded lettuce to eat out of hand. Makes 6 servings.

Per serving: 152 calories, 28 g protein, 5 g carbohydrates, 2 g fat, 0 g saturated fat, 66 mg cholesterol, 861 mg sodium

■ *Pictured on facing page*

CHICKEN JAMBALAYA

Preparation time: About 45 minutes

Baking time: About 45 minutes

When the weather calls for a "tummy warmer," try this Cajun-inspired casserole, heated up with a full tablespoon of pepper.

1 **tablespoon salad oil**

8 **ounces Canadian bacon, diced**

1½ **pounds skinless, boneless chicken breasts, cut into bite-size chunks**

1 **large onion, chopped**

3 **cloves garlic, minced or pressed**

2 **large green bell peppers (about 12 oz.** *total***), seeded and chopped**

1 **cup chopped celery**

6 **large tomatoes (about 2 lbs.** *total***), chopped**

1 **large can (15 oz.) no-salt-added tomato sauce**

2 **dry bay leaves, crumbled**

1 **teaspoon dry thyme leaves**

2 **teaspoons white pepper**

1 **teaspoon ground red pepper (cayenne)**

½ **cup chopped parsley**

1½ **cups long-grain white rice**

3 **cups low-sodium chicken broth**

Heat oil in a 12- to 14-inch frying pan over medium heat. Add Canadian bacon and chicken; cook, stirring often, until browned on all sides (about 6 minutes). Transfer to a 4- to 5-quart casserole.

Add onion, garlic, bell peppers, and celery to pan. Cook, stirring occasionally, until onion is soft (about 10 minutes). Add tomatoes, tomato sauce, bay leaves, thyme, white and red pepper, and parsley; bring to a boil, stirring. Boil gently, uncovered, for 5 minutes.

Pour sauce over chicken; stir in rice and broth. Cover and bake in a 375° oven until rice is tender to bite (about 45 minutes). Makes 6 servings.

Per serving: 472 calories, 42 g protein, 57 g carbohydrates, 8 g fat, 2 g saturated fat, 85 mg cholesterol, 684 mg sodium

Heat up your next party with Chicken Jambalaya (recipe on facing page). Our version of the Cajun classic boasts chunks of chicken breast, bell pepper, tomato, onion, and a tongue-tingling touch of cayenne.

CHICKEN STROGANOFF

Preparation time: About 15 minutes, plus about 1 hour to soak tomatoes

Cooking time: About 25 minutes

Here's an unusual version of a classic company dish. Chicken stands in for beef, rice replaces the traditional noodles, and the sour cream sauce is accented with grated fresh ginger and chopped dried tomatoes. To coat the chicken quickly and easily, shake it together with the flour mixture in a paper or plastic bag.

- ½ **cup dried tomatoes**
- ¼ **cup all-purpose flour**
- ¼ **teaspoon pepper**
- 1 **pound skinless, boneless chicken breasts, cut into ½-inch cubes**
- 3 **tablespoons butter or margarine**
- 3 **tablespoons salad oil**
- 1 **medium-size onion, chopped**
- 8 **ounces mushrooms, sliced**
- 2 **cloves garlic, minced or pressed**
- 1 **teaspoon cornstarch mixed with 2 teaspoons water**
- 1 **cup sour cream**
- ½ **cup regular-strength chicken broth**
- 1 **cup dry white wine**
- ½ **teaspoon *each* grated fresh ginger and dry thyme leaves**
- 2 **tablespoons dry sherry**
  Hot cooked rice
  Chopped parsley

In a small bowl, soak tomatoes in warm water to cover until soft (about 1 hour). Drain well, chop coarsely, and set aside.

In a paper or plastic bag, combine flour and pepper. Shake chicken in bag to coat evenly with flour mixture; shake off excess.

Melt 1½ tablespoons of the butter in 1½ tablespoons of the oil in a 10- to 12-inch frying pan over medium-high heat. Add chicken and cook, stirring often, until no longer pink in center; cut to test (about 5 minutes). Remove from pan with a slotted spoon and set aside.

In pan, melt remaining 1½ tablespoons butter in remaining 1½ tablespoons oil. Add onion, mushrooms, and garlic; cook, stirring often, until mushrooms are lightly browned (about 15 minutes). Meanwhile, stir cornstarch mixture into sour cream.

Stir broth, wine, ginger, thyme, and sherry into pan. Bring to a boil, stirring; then add tomatoes, chicken, and sour cream mixture. Bring to a boil, stirring. Serve over rice and sprinkle with parsley. Makes 4 servings.

Per serving: 512 calories, 32 g protein, 21 g carbohydrates, 33 g fat, 15 g saturated fat, 114 mg cholesterol, 333 mg sodium

STIR-FRIED CHICKEN WITH SORREL

Preparation time: About 20 minutes

Cooking time: About 10 minutes

Fresh sorrel contributes a lemony tartness to this chile-heated stir-fry. Just as appealing as the flavor is the eye-catching medley of colors: white chicken strips, bright greens, and shiny black olives.

- 5 **cups lightly packed sorrel leaves, washed, stems removed**
- 3 **tablespoons salad oil**
- 1 **pound skinless, boneless chicken breasts, cut across the grain into ½-inch-wide strips**
- 3 **cloves garlic, minced or pressed**
- 1 **small onion, chopped**
- ½ **teaspoon crushed dried hot red chiles**
- 1 **can (3½ oz.) pitted ripe olives, drained**
- ¼ **cup grated Parmesan cheese**

Cut sorrel leaves crosswise into 1-inch strips; set aside.

Heat 2 tablespoons of the oil in a wok or 12- to 14-inch frying pan over high heat. Add chicken. Cook, stirring often, until no longer pink in center; cut to test (about 4 minutes). Remove chicken from pan with a slotted spoon and set aside.

Heat remaining 1 tablespoon oil in pan. Add garlic and onion; cook, stirring, until onion is lightly browned (about 4 minutes). Add chiles, olives, and sorrel; cook just until sorrel is wilted. Stir in chicken and 2 tablespoons of the cheese; sprinkle with remaining 2 tablespoons cheese. Makes 4 servings.

Per serving: 283 calories, 29 g protein, 5 g carbohydrates, 16 g fat, 3 g saturated fat, 70 mg cholesterol, 385 mg sodium

CHICKEN BURROS

Preparation time: About 15 minutes

Cooking time: About 25 minutes

Cut into these hot tortilla-wrapped packages and discover a super-satisfying blend of chicken, celery, and mushrooms in a spicy-sweet tomato sauce. Try tossing black beans and bell pepper strips in a simple vinaigrette to serve alongside.

Burro Sauce (recipe follows)

About ½ cup salad oil

1 **clove garlic, minced or pressed**

1 **small dried hot red chile**

8 **ounces skinless, boneless chicken breast, cut into ½-inch cubes**

1 **tablespoon dry sherry**

½ **cup finely chopped celery**

2 **green onions (including tops), thinly sliced**

4 **medium-size mushrooms, sliced**

4 **large flour tortillas (*each* about 10 inches in diameter)**

4 **ounces Cheddar cheese, cut into thin strips**

Prepare Burro Sauce and set aside.

Heat 2 tablespoons of the oil in a 10- to 12-inch frying pan over medium-high heat; add garlic and chile.

Cook, stirring, until chile turns almost black. Discard chile. Add chicken and sherry. Cook, stirring often, until meat is no longer pink in center; cut to test (about 4 minutes). Remove from pan with a slotted spoon and set aside.

Add 1 tablespoon more oil to pan; then add celery and cook, stirring, for 2 minutes. Add onions and mushrooms and cook, stirring, for 2 more minutes. Return chicken to pan, add Burro Sauce, and stir over low heat until hot. Remove from heat.

To shape each burro, lay a tortilla flat. Spoon a fourth of the filling near one edge and top with a fourth of the cheese strips. Fold tortilla edge up over filling, then fold in sides and roll to enclose filling.

Rinse pan and wipe dry. Heat 2 tablespoons more oil in pan over medium-high heat; then add one burro and cook until browned on all sides (about 3 minutes). Remove from pan. Repeat to cook remaining burros, adding remaining oil to pan as needed. Makes 4 servings.

BURRO SAUCE. In a small bowl, stir together ¼ cup **catsup,** 1½ teaspoons **honey,** 1 teaspoon **Worcestershire,** 1 clove **garlic,** minced or pressed, and 2 or 3 drops **liquid hot pepper seasoning.**

Per serving: 573 calories, 25 g protein, 34 g carbohydrates, 38 g fat, 10 g saturated fat, 63 mg cholesterol, 629 mg sodium

GINGER CHICKEN & YAMS

Preparation time: About 30 minutes

Cooking time: About 10 minutes

Candied yams in a stir-fry? That's just about what you get when matchstick strips of yams are cooked with chicken in a gingery brown sugar–sherry sauce. Green and red onions make the dish even more colorful.

Cooking Sauce (recipe follows)

2 **tablespoons olive oil or salad oil**

1 **pound yams, peeled and cut into matchstick-size strips**

1 **small red onion, cut into eighths, layers separated**

1 **pound skinless, boneless chicken breasts, cut into ½-inch cubes**

2 **tablespoons minced fresh ginger**

⅓ **cup minced green onions (including tops)**

Prepare Cooking Sauce and set aside.

Heat 1 tablespoon of the oil in a wok or 12- to 14-inch frying pan over medium heat. Add yams and red onion; cook, stirring often, until vegetables are just tender to bite (about 5 minutes). Spoon onto a platter, cover loosely, and keep warm.

Increase heat to high and heat remaining 1 tablespoon oil in pan. Add chicken and ginger. Cook, stirring often, until meat is no longer pink in center; cut to test (about 4 minutes). Return yams and red onion to pan, add Cooking Sauce, and bring to a boil, stirring. Then stir in green onions and serve. Makes 4 servings.

COOKING SAUCE. In a small bowl, stir together 3 tablespoons *each* **soy sauce, dry sherry,** and **water;** 1 tablespoon firmly packed **brown sugar;** and 1½ teaspoons **cornstarch.**

Per serving: 336 calories, 29 g protein, 36 g carbohydrates, 8 g fat, 1 g saturated fat, 66 mg cholesterol, 857 mg sodium

Chicken in a Squash Shell (recipe on facing page) shows off stir-fried chicken and vegetables in nutty-sweet acorn squash "bowls." For a refreshing accent, top each serving with tart yogurt and a sprinkling of green onions.

CHICKEN IN A SQUASH SHELL

Preparation time: About 25 minutes

Cooking time: About 40 minutes

A sophisticated version of chicken in a basket, this meal is served in acorn squash halves.

> 2 **small acorn squash (about 1 lb. *each*)**
> **Soy-Ginger Sauce (recipe follows)**
> 1 **tablespoon salad oil**
> 1 **pound skinless, boneless chicken breasts, cut into ½-inch cubes**
> 1 **small onion, finely chopped**
> ½ **cup *each* finely diced jicama and red bell pepper**
> 2 **small firm-ripe tomatoes, peeled and finely diced**
> 1 **teaspoon Sichuan peppercorns, toasted (see below) and coarsely ground; or ½ teaspoon black pepper**
> ¼ **cup chopped green onions (including tops)**
> **Plain low-fat yogurt (optional)**

Cut each squash in half lengthwise and scoop out seeds. Place halves, cut side down, in an oiled 9- by 13-inch baking pan. Bake, uncovered, in a 400° oven until tender when pierced (about 40 minutes).

About 20 minutes before squash is done, prepare Soy-Ginger Sauce and set aside. Then heat oil in a wok or 12- to 14-inch frying pan over medium-high heat; add chicken. Cook, stirring often, until meat is no longer pink in center; cut to test (about 5 minutes). Remove from pan with a slotted spoon. Add finely chopped onion, jicama, bell pepper, tomatoes, and peppercorns to pan; cook, stirring often, for 5 minutes. Add sauce and bring to a boil, stirring. Stir in chicken.

Place each squash half in an individual bowl; fill with chicken mixture. Offer green onions and, if desired, yogurt to add to taste. Makes 4 servings.

SOY-GINGER SAUCE. Mix 2 tablespoons *each* **soy sauce** and **dry sherry**; ¾ cup **regular-strength chicken broth**; 1 tablespoon *each* **cornstarch** and firmly packed **brown sugar**; and 1 teaspoon finely minced **fresh ginger.**

Per serving: 283 calories, 30 g protein, 30 g carbohydrates, 5 g fat, 1 g saturated fat, 66 mg cholesterol, 786 mg sodium

CHICKEN WITH CHILI PASTE

Preparation time: About 20 minutes

Cooking time: About 8 minutes

Fragrant ground peppercorns and a paste of crushed chiles provide the heat you expect from a Sichuan stir-fry. Offer rice alongside to temper the fiery flavor.

> **Cooking Sauce (recipe follows)**
> ½ **teaspoon ground toasted Sichuan peppercorns (directions follow)**
> 12 **ounces skinless, boneless chicken breast, cut into 3-inch-long slivers**
> 1 **tablespoon cornstarch**
> 2 **tablespoons rice wine or dry sherry**
> 2 **tablespoons salad oil**
> 2 **tablespoons slivered fresh ginger**
> 1 **tablespoon minced garlic**
> 1½ **to 2 teaspoons chili paste**
> ½ **cup bamboo shoots, cut into slivers**
> 2 **stalks celery, cut into 2-inch-long slivers**

Prepare Cooking Sauce and ground toasted peppercorns; set aside. In a large bowl, mix chicken, cornstarch, and wine. Set aside.

Heat 1 tablespoon of the oil in a wok or 12- to 14-inch frying pan over high heat. Add ginger and garlic; cook, stirring, until garlic is golden. Add chili paste, bamboo shoots, and celery; cook, stirring, for 1 minute. Remove from pan with a slotted spoon.

Heat remaining 1 tablespoon oil in pan; add chicken mixture and cook, stirring often, until chicken is no longer pink (about 2 minutes). Return vegetables to pan, add Cooking Sauce, and stir until sauce boils. Sprinkle with peppercorns. Makes 3 servings.

COOKING SAUCE. Mix 2 tablespoons **rice wine** or dry sherry, 1 tablespoon **soy sauce**, 1 tablespoon **rice vinegar** or white wine vinegar, and 1 teaspoon *each* **sugar, Oriental sesame oil,** and **cornstarch.**

GROUND TOASTED SICHUAN PEPPERCORNS. Place 1 tablespoon **Sichuan peppercorns** in a 6- to 8-inch frying pan. Pick out and discard any debris. Cook over medium heat until peppercorns are fragrant and lightly toasted (about 3 minutes), shaking pan often. Finely crush with a mortar and pestle (or whirl in a blender). Makes 2 teaspoons.

Per serving: 282 calories, 28 g protein, 15 g carbohydrates, 12 g fat, 2 g saturated fat, 66 mg cholesterol, 521 mg sodium

MICROWAVE MATCHUPS

If you have a microwave oven, you have just the help you need to put dinner on the table extra-fast. Cooking takes mere minutes; cleanup is usually quicker, too. Microwaved meals also offer health benefits: nutrients are retained well, and you can often use less fat than you would for conventional cooking.

As the recipes on these pages prove, poultry takes especially well to microwaving. Try chicken breasts topped with capers and anchovies, or enjoy mustard-sauced dark meat over hot vermicelli. When the occasion calls for something fancy, serve tender turkey steaks wrapped around a creamy spinach filling. Or choose turkey tenderloins masked in a rich-tasting raspberry glaze made without a bit of oil or butter.

CHICKEN BREASTS WITH ANCHOVIES & RED PEPPERS

Preparation time: About 5 minutes

Marinating time: At least 30 minutes or up to 4 hours

Microwaving time: About 10 minutes

Standing time: 2 minutes

> 6 skinless, boneless chicken breast halves (about 1½ lbs. *total*)
> ¼ cup dry vermouth
> 2 tablespoons olive oil
> 1 tablespoon lemon juice
> ½ teaspoon grated lemon peel
> 1 clove garlic, minced or pressed
> 1 small red bell pepper, seeded and cut into thin strips
> 6 canned flat anchovy fillets, drained and coarsely chopped
> 1 teaspoon drained capers
> 1 tablespoon chopped parsley

Rinse chicken and pat dry. In a wide, shallow bowl, stir together vermouth, oil, lemon juice, lemon peel, and garlic. Add chicken and turn to coat; then cover

and refrigerate for at least 30 minutes or up to 4 hours. Drain chicken; reserve marinade.

In a 10- to 11-inch microwave-safe baking dish, arrange chicken in a single layer, positioning thickest parts of breasts toward outside of dish. Cover and microwave on **HIGH (100%)** for about 6 minutes, giving dish a quarter-turn every 1½ minutes. Let stand, covered, for 2 minutes. Meat in thickest part should no longer be pink; cut to test. Remove chicken from dish and set aside.

Add marinade and bell pepper to dish. Microwave, uncovered, on **HIGH (100%)** for 3 minutes or until pepper is tender-crisp to bite, stirring every minute. Return chicken to dish, arranging it in a single layer; spoon sauce and peppers up over chicken. Sprinkle with anchovies and capers. Microwave, uncovered, on **HIGH (100%)** for 1 minute or until heated through. Sprinkle with parsley. Makes 6 servings.

Per serving: 182 calories, 27 g protein, 2 g carbohydrates, 6 g fat, 1 g saturated fat, 68 mg cholesterol, 235 mg sodium

MUSTARD CHICKEN CHUNKS WITH VERMICELLI

Preparation time: About 5 minutes

Microwaving time: About 17 minutes

> 1½ pounds boneless chicken thighs, skinned
> 1½ tablespoons butter or margarine
> 1 small clove garlic, minced or pressed
> 1 teaspoon mustard seeds, coarsely crushed
> ¼ teaspoon dry tarragon leaves
> ⅓ cup dry white wine
> 2 teaspoons Dijon mustard
> ¼ cup sliced green onions (including tops)
> ½ cup sour cream
> 8 to 10 ounces dry vermicelli, cooked according to package directions and drained (keep hot)

Rinse chicken and pat dry. Preheat a 2- to 2½-quart or 10-inch-square microwave browning dish on **HIGH (100%)** for 4½ minutes. Using oven mitts, carefully remove dish to a heatproof surface. Add butter; swirl dish to coat bottom with butter. Immediately add chicken thighs in a single layer. Wait until sizzling stops; then turn chicken over and sprinkle evenly with garlic, mustard seeds, and tarragon. Cover and microwave on **HIGH (100%)** for 5 minutes, giving dish a half-turn after 2½ minutes. Meat in thickest part should no longer be pink; cut to test. Remove chicken from dish and set aside.

Stir wine and mustard into liquid in dish. Microwave, uncovered, on **HIGH (100%)** for 5 minutes or until mixture comes to a boil and browns slightly at edges.

Return chicken to dish; stir in onions and sour cream. Microwave, uncovered, on **HIGH (100%)** for 2 minutes or until sauce is heated through, stirring after 1 minute. Serve over hot cooked vermicelli. Makes 4 servings.

Per serving: 493 calories, 34 g protein, 50 g carbohydrates, 17 g fat, 8 g saturated fat, 126 mg cholesterol, 246 mg sodium

FLORENTINE TURKEY ROLLS

Preparation time: About 15 minutes

Microwaving time: About 22 minutes

- 1½ **tablespoons butter or margarine**
- 4 **ounces mushrooms, thinly sliced**
- 1½ **tablespoons all-purpose flour**
- ⅛ **teaspoon** *each* **ground nutmeg and white pepper**
- ½ **cup** *each* **regular-strength chicken broth, dry white wine, and half-and-half**
- 4 **turkey breast steaks (about 5 oz.** *each*), cut ½ inch thick
- 1 **package (10 oz.) frozen chopped spinach, thawed and squeezed dry**
- 1½ **cups (6 oz.) shredded Swiss cheese**

Place butter in a shallow 2- to 2½-quart microwave-safe baking dish. Microwave, uncovered, on **HIGH (100%)** for 30 to 35 seconds or until butter is melted. Add mushrooms and stir to coat with butter. Microwave, uncovered, on **HIGH (100%)** for 3 minutes, stirring once. Blend flour, nutmeg, and pepper into mushroom mixture. Gradually stir in broth, wine, and half-and-half to make a smooth sauce. Microwave, uncovered, on **HIGH (100%)** for 6 minutes or until sauce boils and thickens, stirring every 2 minutes.

Rinse turkey and pat dry. Place each steak between 2 sheets of plastic wrap; pound with a flat-surfaced mallet to a thickness of about ¼ inch.

In a bowl, mix spinach, 1 cup of the cheese, and 3 tablespoons of the mushroom sauce. Place a fourth of the filling at one end of each pounded turkey steak; roll to enclose. Place rolls, seam side down, in remaining sauce in baking dish; spoon some of the sauce up over rolls.

Cover and microwave on **HIGH (100%)** for 5 minutes. Rearrange rolls, bringing those in center to ends of dish; cover and microwave on **HIGH (100%)** for 5 minutes. Sprinkle remaining ½ cup cheese over rolls. Microwave, uncovered, on **HIGH (100%)** for 2 minutes or until cheese is melted and turkey is no longer pink; cut to test.

To serve, place one roll on each of 4 dinner plates. Cut each roll diagonally into ½-inch-thick slices; then arrange slices on plates so stuffing shows. Spoon a fourth of the sauce over and around each serving. Makes 4 servings.

Per serving: 438 calories, 50 g protein, 10 g carbohydrates, 22 g fat, 13 g saturated fat, 150 mg cholesterol, 440 mg sodium

RASPBERRY-GLAZED TURKEY TENDERLOINS

Preparation time: About 5 minutes

Microwaving time: 6 to 7 minutes

- 2 **turkey breast tenderloins (about 6 oz.** *each*)
- ¼ **cup seedless red raspberry jam**
- 3 **tablespoons raspberry vinegar**
- 2 **tablespoons Dijon mustard**
- 1 **teaspoon grated orange peel**
- ¼ **teaspoon dry thyme leaves**
  Salt

Rinse turkey and pat dry. In a shallow 2- to 2½-quart microwave-safe baking dish, stir together jam, vinegar, mustard, orange peel, and thyme until well blended. Add turkey; turn to coat well with sauce.

Cover and microwave on **HIGH (100%)** for 3 minutes. Brush turkey with sauce; then arrange with uncooked portions toward outside of dish. Microwave, uncovered, on **HIGH (100%)** for 3 to 4 minutes or until meat in thickest part is no longer pink; cut to test. Season to taste with salt. Makes 2 servings.

Per serving: 325 calories, 40 g protein, 32 g carbohydrates, 4 g fat, 1 g saturated fat, 105 mg cholesterol, 569 mg sodium

CHICKEN ON A STICK WITH COUSCOUS

Preparation time: About 30 minutes

Marinating time: At least 30 minutes or up to 4 hours

Grilling time: About 10 minutes

Cut the heat of a summer afternoon with this quick-cooking barbecue. You can thread the chicken on metal or bamboo skewers; if you choose bamboo skewers, soak them in hot water for 30 minutes before grilling.

> **Cumin-Garlic-Yogurt Sauce (recipe follows)**
> ⅓ **cup lemon juice**
> ⅓ **cup olive oil or salad oil**
> ¼ **cup dry white wine**
> 6 **cloves garlic, minced or pressed**
> 2 **dry bay leaves, crumbled**
> 1¼ **pounds skinless, boneless chicken breasts, cut into ¾-inch cubes**
> 2½ **cups low-sodium chicken broth**
> 1¾ **cups couscous**
> ½ **cup sliced green onions (including tops)**
> **Salt and pepper**

Prepare Cumin-Garlic-Yogurt Sauce; refrigerate. In a bowl, combine lemon juice, oil, wine, garlic, and bay leaves. Add chicken, stir to coat, cover, and refrigerate for at least 30 minutes or up to 4 hours.

Lift chicken from marinade and drain briefly; reserve marinade. Thread chicken equally on 8 metal skewers. Place chicken on a lightly greased grill 4 to 6 inches above a solid bed of medium-hot coals. Cook, basting with marinade and turning as needed, until meat is lightly browned on outside and no longer pink in center; cut to test (about 10 minutes).

Meanwhile, in a 2- to 3-quart pan, bring broth to a boil over medium-high heat; stir in couscous. Cover, remove from heat, and let stand until liquid is absorbed (about 5 minutes). Stir in onions; season to taste with salt and pepper.

To serve, fluff couscous with a fork; then spoon couscous onto a platter and top with chicken skewers. Serve with sauce to add to taste. Makes 4 servings.

Per serving without sauce: 553 calories, 44 g protein, 63 g carbohydrates, 12 g fat, 2 g saturated fat, 82 mg cholesterol, 137 mg sodium

CUMIN-GARLIC-YOGURT SAUCE. In a bowl, stir together 1½ cups **plain low-fat yogurt;** 2 tablespoons minced **fresh cilantro** (coriander); 1 clove **garlic,** minced or pressed; and 1 teaspoon **cumin seeds.** Cover and refrigerate for at least 15 minutes or until next day. Makes about 1½ cups.

Per tablespoon: 9 calories, 1 g protein, 1 g carbohydrates, 0 g fat, 0 g saturated fat, 1 mg cholesterol, 10 mg sodium

CHILI CHICKEN CHUNKS

Preparation time: About 20 minutes

Cooking time: About 15 minutes

Chips are the usual dippers for guacamole, but chicken chunks do just as well. Coat the meat in a spicy, cornmeal-crunchy beer batter before frying.

> ¾ **cup all-purpose flour**
> ¼ **cup yellow cornmeal**
> 2 **teaspoons chili powder**
> ½ **teaspoon *each* paprika and salt**
> ¼ **teaspoon *each* ground cumin and dry oregano leaves**
> ⅛ **teaspoon pepper**
> ¾ **cup beer**
> 1½ **pounds skinless, boneless chicken breasts, cut into 1½-inch chunks**
> **Salad oil**
> **Homemade or purchased guacamole**

In a bowl, mix flour, cornmeal, chili powder, paprika, salt, cumin, oregano, and pepper. Add beer and stir until smooth. Add chicken pieces to batter and stir to coat evenly.

In a deep 3- to 4-quart pan, heat 1 to 1½ inches of oil to 350°F on a deep-frying thermometer. Lift chicken from batter, a piece at a time, and add to oil. Fill pan with a single layer of chicken; do not crowd pan. Cook, stirring occasionally, until chicken is richly browned on outside and no longer pink in center; cut to test (about 2 minutes). As chicken is cooked, lift it from pan with a slotted spoon; drain on paper towels.

To serve, mound chicken in a napkin-lined basket; offer guacamole alongside. Makes 8 to 10 servings.

Per serving: 194 calories, 19 g protein, 12 g carbohydrates, 7 g fat, 1 g saturated fat, 44 mg cholesterol, 178 mg sodium

Dinner will be off the grill and on the table in no time when you prepare Chicken on a Stick with Couscous (recipe on facing page). The garlicky barbecued chicken chunks are served with a cool, cilantro-seasoned yogurt sauce.

FAJITA CHICKEN SKEWERS

Preparation time: About 15 minutes

Marinating time: At least 1 hour or up to 8 hours

Grilling time: About 10 minutes

Fajitas come off the grill faster if you start with marinated chicken chunks. Don't let the amount of spices scare you; the seasonings flavor the meat perfectly.

- ½ cup *each* lime juice and salad oil
- ¼ cup *each* beer and firmly packed brown sugar
- 1 large onion, thinly sliced
- 1 clove garlic, minced or pressed
- 2 fresh jalapeño chiles, seeded and minced
- 2 tablespoons *each* ground cumin and paprika
- 1 tablespoon Worcestershire
- 1 teaspoon pepper
- 1 pound skinless, boneless chicken breasts, cut into ¾-inch cubes
- 8 flour tortillas (*each* about 8 inches in diameter)

Shredded Cheddar cheese, homemade or purchased guacamole, and sour cream (optional)

In a large bowl, combine lime juice, oil, beer, sugar, onion, garlic, chiles, cumin, paprika, Worcestershire, and pepper. Add chicken and stir to coat; cover and refrigerate for at least 1 hour or up to 8 hours.

Drain chicken; discard marinade. Thread chicken equally on 4 metal skewers. Sprinkle each tortilla with a few drops of water; then stack tortillas and wrap in heavy-duty foil.

Place chicken on a lightly greased grill 4 to 6 inches above a solid bed of hot coals. Place tortillas at edge of grill (not above coals). Cook, turning chicken and tortillas occasionally, until tortillas are warm and chicken is lightly browned on outside and no longer pink in center; cut to test (about 10 minutes).

To eat, place chicken on a tortilla; top with cheese, guacamole, and sour cream, if desired. Roll to enclose, then eat out of hand. Makes 4 servings.

Per serving: 440 calories, 33 g protein, 54 g carbohydrates, 9 g fat, 1 g saturated fat, 66 mg cholesterol, 507 mg sodium

CHICKEN & WATERMELON WITH HERBS

Preparation time: About 25 minutes

Marinating time: 1 to 2 hours

Grilling time: About 12 minutes

Grilled chicken shares the spotlight—as well as a minty orange sauce—with skewers of crisp, juicy melon. Cook and company alike will appreciate the small, almost seedless, red- or yellow-fleshed watermelons now available in many markets.

Orange-Herb Sauce (recipe follows)
- ⅓ cup orange juice
- 1 teaspoon ground coriander
- 2 pounds skinless, boneless chicken breasts, cut into 1½-inch cubes
- 1 piece seedless or seed-in watermelon (about 2 lbs.), rind removed

Salt and pepper

Prepare Orange-Herb Sauce and refrigerate.

In a bowl, mix orange juice and coriander. Add chicken, stir to coat, cover, and refrigerate for 1 to 2 hours. Drain chicken, discarding marinade; thread chicken equally on 8 metal skewers. Cut watermelon into 1-inch cubes; thread equally on 8 skewers.

Place chicken on a lightly greased grill 4 to 6 inches above a solid bed of hot coals. Cook, turning as needed, until lightly browned on outside and no longer pink in center; cut to test (about 12 minutes).

Arrange chicken and watermelon on individual plates; offer Orange-Herb Sauce to pour over meat and fruit. Makes 8 servings.

Per serving without sauce: 146 calories, 27 g protein, 5 g carbohydrates, 2 g fat, 0 g saturated fat, 66 mg cholesterol, 75 mg sodium

ORANGE-HERB SAUCE. In a small bowl, stir together 1 cup **orange juice**; ½ teaspoon grated **orange peel**; 1 clove **garlic,** minced or pressed; 1 tablespoon finely chopped **fresh mint** or dry mint leaves; 1 tablespoon finely chopped **fresh dill** or 1 teaspoon dry dill weed; 1 tablespoon finely chopped **fresh cilantro** (coriander); and 1 tablespoon **balsamic vinegar** or red wine vinegar. Makes about 1¼ cups.

Per tablespoon: 6 calories, 0 g protein, 1 g carbohydrates, 0 g fat, 0 g saturated fat, 0 mg cholesterol, 0 mg sodium

YAKITORI CHICKEN & VEGETABLES

Preparation time: About 20 minutes

Marinating time: At least 1 hour or up to 8 hours

Grilling time: About 30 minutes

A simple soy marinade, nippy with fresh ginger, seasons every part of this meal—skewered chicken chunks, fresh shiitake mushrooms, and slender Oriental eggplants. Slash the eggplants before grilling so the flavors can really sink in.

2 **tablespoons sesame seeds**

1 **pound skinless, boneless chicken breasts, cut into ¾-inch cubes**

Sherry-Soy Marinade (recipe follows)

6 **medium-size Oriental eggplants**

18 **large fresh shiitake mushrooms or button mushrooms**

Toast sesame seeds in a small frying pan over medium heat until golden (about 3 minutes), shaking pan often. Set aside.

Place chicken in a bowl. Prepare Sherry-Soy Marinade; pour ¼ cup of the marinade over chicken and mix gently to coat (reserve remaining marinade). Cover and refrigerate for at least 1 hour or up to 8 hours.

Drain chicken; discard any marinade left in bowl. Thread chicken equally on 6 metal skewers. Set aside.

Slash each eggplant lengthwise or crosswise in 4 or 5 places, making cuts ⅓ inch deep and spacing them evenly. Cut mushroom stems flush with caps.

Place eggplants on a lightly greased grill 4 to 6 inches above a solid bed of hot coals. Cook, turning often, until eggplants are slightly charred and very soft when pressed (about 30 minutes).

After eggplants have cooked for 20 minutes, start cooking mushrooms and chicken. Dip mushrooms in reserved marinade, drain briefly, and set on grill. Cook for 5 minutes; turn over and continue to cook until softened and lightly browned (about 5 more minutes). At the same time you place mushrooms on grill, place chicken on grill and cook, turning as needed, until meat is lightly browned on outside and no longer pink in center; cut to test (about 10 minutes).

Arrange chicken, mushrooms, and eggplants on a shallow platter. Pull each eggplant apart at a slash to expose flesh. Moisten chicken and vegetables with marinade and sprinkle with sesame seeds. Pass any remaining marinade at the table. Makes 6 servings.

SHERRY-SOY MARINADE. In a small bowl, stir together ⅓ cup **dry sherry**, 3 tablespoons *each* **soy sauce** and **Oriental sesame oil,** and 1½ teaspoons finely minced **fresh ginger.**

Per serving: 252 calories, 23 g protein, 21 g carbohydrates, 10 g fat, 1 g saturated fat, 44 mg cholesterol, 578 mg sodium

BARBECUED CHICKEN & POTATO KEBABS

Preparation time: About 45 minutes

Grilling time: About 12 minutes

Here's a hearty and unusual version of chicken on a stick. Cubed chicken, precooked small potatoes, and mushrooms are threaded on skewers and basted with homemade barbecue sauce as they grill.

1 **tablespoon salad oil**

1 **medium-size onion, chopped**

1 **clove garlic, minced or pressed**

1 **can (8 oz.) tomato sauce**

½ **cup red wine vinegar**

¼ **cup firmly packed brown sugar**

1 **tablespoon Worcestershire**

8 **small red thin-skinned potatoes (*each* 1½ to 2 inches in diameter), scrubbed**

24 **mushrooms (about 1 lb. *total*)**

1 **pound skinless, boneless chicken breasts, cut into 1½-inch cubes**

Heat oil in a 3-quart pan over medium heat. Add onion and garlic; cook, stirring often, until onion is soft (about 10 minutes). Add tomato sauce, vinegar, sugar, and Worcestershire. Bring to a boil; then reduce heat and simmer, uncovered, until thickened (about 20 minutes), stirring occasionally to prevent sauce from sticking.

Meanwhile, cook potatoes in boiling water to cover until barely tender when pierced (about 10 minutes); drain.

Thread potatoes, mushrooms, and chicken equally on 4 sturdy metal skewers. Place skewers on a lightly greased grill 4 to 6 inches above a solid bed of hot coals. Cook, turning as needed and basting several times with sauce, until meat is longer pink in center; cut to test (about 12 minutes). Makes 4 servings.

Per serving: 347 calories, 32 g protein, 44 g carbohydrates, 6 g fat, 1 g saturated fat, 66 mg cholesterol, 475 mg sodium

Roast Turkey Breast with Dried Fruit & Cranberries (recipe on facing page) is a perfect meal for a brisk fall day. Choose your favorite dried fruit for the sauce; we opted for apricot halves. Braised leeks and puréed winter squash complete the feast.

ROAST TURKEY BREAST WITH DRIED FRUIT & CRANBERRIES

Preparation time: About 10 minutes

Roasting time: About 1 hour

A turkey breast half is just the right size to feed a hungry group of six. To complement the meat, choose dried apricots, peaches, prunes, or figs; or use some of each kind.

1 turkey breast half (about 3 lbs.)

1 pound (about 2 cups) dried apricots, peaches, pitted prunes, or figs; or use a combination

1 cup apple juice

1 cup low-sodium chicken broth

1 cup fresh or frozen cranberries

2 tablespoons firmly packed brown sugar

Rinse turkey and pat dry. Place, skin side up, in a 9-by 13-inch baking pan. Surround with dried fruit; pour apple juice over fruit. Tightly cover pan with foil. Roast in a 400° oven for 40 minutes. Uncover; add broth and cranberries to pan, then sprinkle in 1 tablespoon of the sugar. Continue to roast, uncovered, basting turkey with pan juices 2 or 3 times, until meat in thickest part is no longer pink; cut to test (about 20 more minutes).

Transfer turkey to a platter; with a slotted spoon, arrange fruit around meat. Add remaining 1 tablespoon sugar to pan juices; boil over medium-high heat until sauce is thickened (about 5 minutes). Spoon sauce over turkey and fruit. Makes 6 servings.

Per serving: 550 calories, 48 g protein, 58 g carbohydrates, 15 g fat, 4 g saturated fat, 133 mg cholesterol, 249 mg sodium

TURKEY ROAST WITH HERB HEART

Preparation time: About 20 minutes

Roasting time: About 2 hours

Looking for an elegant entrée that doesn't require hours of effort? Layer fresh parsley, thyme, fontina cheese, and prosciutto over a boned turkey breast; then fold the meat around the filling, tie it to secure, and slip it into the oven. The result is a richly flavored roast with an aromatic "heart" of green herbs.

1 boned turkey breast (about 4 lbs.)

¼ cup chopped parsley

2 tablespoons minced fresh thyme leaves or 2 teaspoons dry thyme leaves

Salt and pepper

2 ounces *each* thinly sliced fontina cheese and thinly sliced prosciutto

3 or 4 thyme or parsley sprigs (*each* 3 to 4 inches long)

1⅓ cups regular-strength chicken broth

½ cup dry white wine

1½ tablespoons cornstarch mixed with 3 tablespoons water

On a board, lay three 18-inch-long pieces of cotton string parallel to each other and about 2 inches apart. Rinse turkey and pat dry; then place turkey atop strings, setting it skin side down and perpendicular to strings.

Sprinkle turkey evenly with parsley, minced thyme, salt, and pepper. Lay cheese and prosciutto over surface, overlapping slices. Fold over one side of breast; then turn whole breast over, so top side faces up. Tuck any excess skin underneath.

Arrange thyme sprigs on top of turkey. Bring ends of strings over turkey and tie to secure. Then cut a few more strings and tie turkey roast lengthwise a few times to make neat and compact.

Place roast, skin side up, on a rack in a 12- by 15-inch roasting pan. Roast, uncovered, in a 325° oven until meat in thickest part is no longer pink; cut to test (about 2 hours). Transfer turkey to a platter and remove strings. Let rest for about 15 minutes (keep warm).

Add broth and wine to drippings in roasting pan. Set over high heat and stir to scrape up browned bits; add cornstarch mixture and bring to a boil, stirring. Offer sauce to spoon over sliced meat. Makes 8 to 10 servings.

Per serving without sauce: 300 calories, 43 g protein, 1 g carbohydrates, 13 g fat, 4 g saturated fat, 113 mg cholesterol, 276 mg sodium

Per tablespoon sauce: 3 calories, 0 g protein, 0 g carbohydrates, 0 g fat, 0 g saturated fat, 0 mg cholesterol, 41 mg sodium

TURKEY TONNATO

Preparation time: About 15 minutes

Roasting time: About 2 hours

Chilling time: At least 4 hours or up to 2 days

Terrific when the temperature soars, this version of an Italian classic features cold turkey with a rich, creamy tuna-caper sauce. It's the perfect make-ahead meal; you can prepare both meat and sauce early in the morning or even a few days in advance.

- 1 **boned, rolled, and tied turkey breast (about 4 lbs.)**
- 1 **small onion, finely chopped**
- ½ **cup dry white wine**
- 2 **tablespoons butter or margarine, melted**
  Tonnato Sauce (recipe follows)
- 4 **hard-cooked eggs, halved**
- 4 **medium-size tomatoes, cut into wedges**
  Watercress sprigs

Rinse turkey and pat dry; place, skin side up, in a shallow roasting pan. In a small bowl, mix onion, wine, and butter; pour over turkey. Roast turkey, uncovered, in a 325° oven until meat in thickest part is no longer pink; cut to test (about 2 hours).

Transfer turkey from pan to a plate; reserve pan drippings. Let turkey cool; then cover and refrigerate for at least 4 hours or up to 2 days.

Meanwhile, skim and discard fat from pan drippings. Stir to scrape up browned bits, then pour drippings into a measuring cup. Add water, if needed, to make ½ cup. Use drippings to prepare Tonnato Sauce.

To serve, remove strings and skin from turkey. Thinly slice meat and arrange on a platter; garnish with eggs, tomatoes, and watercress. Offer Tonnato Sauce to add to taste. Makes 8 to 10 servings.

Per serving without sauce: 251 calories, 46 g protein, 3 g carbohydrates, 5 g fat, 2 g saturated fat, 217 mg cholesterol, 120 mg sodium

TONNATO SAUCE. In a blender or food processor, combine the ½ cup **drippings;** 1 can (about 7 oz.) **oil-packed tuna,** drained; 2 tablespoons *each* drained **capers** and **lemon juice;** and 1 clove **garlic,** halved. Whirl until puréed. Pour sauce into a bowl, cover, and refrigerate for at least 4 hours or up to 2 days. Makes about 1½ cups.

Per tablespoon: 21 calories, 2 g protein, 0 g carbohydrates, 1 g fat, 0 g saturated fat, 3 mg cholesterol, 51 mg sodium

STEAMED TURKEY BREAST WITH HERB MAYONNAISE

Preparation time: About 15 minutes

Cooking time: About 1½ hours

Chilling time: At least 4 hours or up to 2 days

Moist, tender turkey—the product of careful steaming—makes a simple supper or super sandwiches. Serve the juicy meat with our Green Herb Mayonnaise, easily made by blending purchased mayonnaise with watercress, parsley, and green onions.

- 1 **turkey breast half (about 3 lbs.)**
- 6 **parsley sprigs**
- 1 **small onion, thinly sliced**
  Green Herb Mayonnaise (recipe follows)

Tear or cut a sheet of heavy-duty foil large enough to enclose turkey. Rinse turkey, pat dry, and place, skin side up, on foil. Top turkey with parsley and onion; wrap in foil. Place on a rack in a large pan above 1 to 2 inches of boiling water. Cover and steam (adding water, if necessary) until meat near bone is no longer pink; cut to test (about 1½ hours).

Meanwhile, prepare Green Herb Mayonnaise.

Remove turkey from pan; unwrap completely. Discard parsley and onion. When turkey is cool enough to handle, remove skin and bones. Cover turkey and refrigerate for at least 4 hours or up to 2 days.

To serve, thinly slice turkey and arrange on a platter. Offer Green Herb Mayonnaise to add to taste. Makes 6 servings.

Per serving without mayonnaise: 290 calories, 56 g protein, 0 g carbohydrates, 6 g fat, 2 g saturated fat, 130 mg cholesterol, 128 mg sodium

GREEN HERB MAYONNAISE. In a food processor, combine 1 cup *each* lightly packed **watercress sprigs** and **parsley sprigs;** ⅓ cup sliced **green onions** (including tops); 1 clove **garlic;** and ¼ teaspoon **dry rosemary.** Whirl until minced. (Or mince watercress, parsley, onions, and garlic; add rosemary.) Blend in ½ cup **mayonnaise.** Cover and refrigerate for at least 30 minutes or up to 2 days. Makes about 1¼ cups.

Per tablespoon: 42 calories, 0 g protein, 1 g carbohydrates, 4 g fat, 1 g saturated fat, 3 mg cholesterol, 34 mg sodium

BARBECUED TURKEY BREAST WITH PEACHES & CHUTNEY

Preparation time: 15 minutes, plus 30 minutes to heat coals

Grilling time: About 1¼ hours

Forget the expected at your next barbecue. Instead of the usual hamburgers, hot dogs, and steaks, offer up a succulent boneless turkey breast glazed with puréed chutney. The green onions and fresh peaches that grill alongside the turkey are another delightful surprise.

⅔ **cup Major Grey's chutney**

1 **teaspoon minced fresh ginger**

1 **turkey breast half (about 3 lbs.), skinned and boned**

3 **firm-ripe fresh peaches; or 6 canned peach halves, drained**

2 **tablespoons lemon juice (if using fresh peaches)**

6 **to 8 green onions**

Salt

Prepare a covered barbecue for grilling by indirect heat as directed for Barbecued Turkey on page 22.

In a blender, whirl ⅓ cup of the chutney with ginger until smoothly puréed. Coarsely chop remaining ⅓ cup chutney and set aside. Rinse turkey, pat dry, and brush all over with some of the puréed chutney.

Place turkey on lightly greased grill directly above drip pan. Cover barbecue and adjust dampers as necessary to maintain an even heat. Cook, brushing occasionally with puréed chutney, until meat in thickest part is no longer pink; cut to test (about 1¼ hours).

Meanwhile, immerse fresh peaches in boiling water for about 30 seconds; lift from water and let cool for 1 minute. Peel, halve, and pit; then coat with lemon juice to prevent darkening. Cut root ends from onions, peel off outer layer, and trim tops, leaving about 4 inches of green leaves.

About 10 minutes before turkey is done, lay peach halves (cut side down) and onions on grill over coals. Cook, turning once and brushing several times with puréed chutney, until peaches are hot and onion tops are wilted (about 10 minutes).

Arrange turkey on a platter; surround with peaches and onions. Slice meat and serve with chopped chutney; season to taste with salt. Makes 6 servings.

Per serving: 282 calories, 35 g protein, 27 g carbohydrates, 3 g fat, 1 g saturated fat, 78 mg cholesterol, 140 mg sodium

BARBECUED TURKEY SALTIMBOCCA

Preparation time: About 15 minutes

Grilling time: About 6 minutes

The aroma of fresh sage can attract a crowd in record time. Fortunately, these ham- and cheese-topped turkey slices can be grilled in mere minutes, allowing the cook to pacify any hungry hordes quickly.

1 **turkey breast half (about 3 lbs.), skinned and boned**

1 **large clove garlic, cut in half**

2 **teaspoons olive oil**

20 **large fresh sage leaves**

4 **ounces thinly sliced prosciutto**

4 **ounces thinly sliced Swiss cheese**

Rinse turkey, pat dry, and cut across the grain into 10 slices, each about ½ inch thick. Rub each slice all over with cut garlic, then rub with oil. Press one sage leaf onto one side of each turkey slice. Cut prosciutto and cheese into equal-size pieces; you need one prosciutto slice and one cheese slice for each turkey slice. Set aside.

Place turkey, sage side up, on a lightly greased grill 4 to 6 inches above a solid bed of hot coals. Cook for 3 minutes, then turn slices over. Quickly top each piece with a slice of prosciutto, a slice of cheese, and another sage leaf. Cover barbecue and adjust dampers (or cover with a tent of heavy-duty foil). Continue to cook until meat is no longer pink in center; cut to test (about 3 more minutes). Using a wide metal spatula, transfer turkey to individual plates. Makes 5 servings.

Per serving: 355 calories, 52 g protein, 2 g carbohydrates, 14 g fat, 6 g saturated fat, 128 mg cholesterol, 648 mg sodium

CREAMY PESTO TURKEY

Preparation time: About 20 minutes

Cooking time: About 20 minutes

When you deserve a treat, there's no better reward than this rich combination of pasta, turkey, and pine nuts in a creamy basil-scented sauce.

- 3 tablespoons pine nuts
  Pesto Sauce (recipe follows)
- 8 ounces dry shell-shaped pasta
- 1 tablespoon olive oil
- 1 pound skinless, boneless turkey breast, cut into ¼- by 2-inch strips
- ¼ cup dry white wine
- 1 cup whipping cream
- ¼ teaspoon ground nutmeg

Toast pine nuts in a small frying pan over medium-low heat until lightly browned (about 3 minutes), shaking pan often. Prepare Pesto Sauce, using 2 tablespoons of the pine nuts; set Pesto Sauce and remaining 1 tablespoon pine nuts aside.

Cook pasta according to package directions just until tender to bite. Drain well and set aside.

Heat oil in a 12- to 14-inch frying pan over medium-high heat. Add turkey and cook, stirring often, until no longer pink in center; cut to test (about 3 minutes). Remove turkey from pan and set aside. Add Pesto Sauce and wine to pan; cook over medium heat, stirring occasionally, until bubbly (about 2 minutes). Stir in cream and bring to a full rolling boil, stirring often. Add nutmeg, pasta, and turkey; mix lightly and sprinkle with remaining 1 tablespoon pine nuts. Makes 4 servings.

PESTO SAUCE. In a blender or food processor, combine 2 tablespoons **toasted pine nuts;** 1 clove **garlic,** coarsely chopped; 1 cup lightly packed **fresh basil leaves;** ¼ cup grated **Parmesan cheese;** 2 tablespoons **olive oil;** and ¼ cup **butter.** Whirl until well combined, scraping sides of container several times.

Per serving: 800 calories, 41 g protein, 49 g carbohydrates, 50 g fat, 23 g saturated fat, 172 mg cholesterol, 313 mg sodium

WESTERN TURKEY CASSEROLE

Preparation time: About 15 minutes

Baking time: About 40 minutes

Here's a savory Southwestern-style meal that's sure to warm up a chilly evening. Layers of green chiles, spicy sautéed turkey, and cheese custard add up to a hearty one-dish dinner.

- 2 tablespoons salad oil
- 1 pound skinless, boneless turkey breast, cut into ¼- by 2-inch strips
- 1 small onion, chopped
- 1 cup prepared taco sauce
- 2 cups (8 oz.) shredded jack cheese
- ¼ cup all-purpose flour
- 4 large eggs
- ¾ cup milk
- 2 large cans (7 oz. *each*) whole green chiles

Heat oil in a 10- to 12-inch frying pan over medium heat; add turkey and onion. Cook, stirring often, until turkey is white on outside but still pink in center; cut to test (about 5 minutes). Stir in taco sauce, remove from heat, and set aside.

In a bowl, mix cheese and flour; then beat in eggs and milk. Slice chiles open and remove any seeds.

Cover bottom of a greased shallow 9-inch-square baking dish with half the chiles. Top with half the turkey mixture, then half the cheese mixture. Repeat layers, using remaining ingredients.

Bake, uncovered, in a 350° oven until golden brown on top (about 40 minutes). Let stand for about 5 minutes before serving. Makes 6 servings.

Per serving: 389 calories, 33 g protein, 15 g carbohydrates, 22 g fat, 3 g saturated fat, 226 mg cholesterol, 1,008 mg sodium

Classic pesto sauce, turkey breast, pasta seashells, pine nuts, and
cream add up to a deliciously memorable treat. Serve Creamy Pesto Turkey
(recipe on facing page) with ripe cherry tomatoes—first heated in olive oil with
tender sautéed garlic cloves, then sprinkled with Italian parsley.

TURKEY CURRY

Preparation time: About 20 minutes

Cooking time: About 15 minutes

Create your own curry powder with a fragrant blend of seasonings, including ginger, chiles, coriander, cumin, and fennel—then use it to season tender turkey breast strips. Add cream and broth, serve over rice, and top with crunchy cashews for a flavorful treat.

>   2 **tablespoons salad oil**
> ¼ **cup minced shallots**
>   1 **clove garlic, minced or pressed**
>   1 **tablespoon grated fresh ginger**
>   1 **teaspoon *each* crushed dried hot red chiles, ground coriander, ground cumin, and ground turmeric**
> ½ **teaspoon fennel seeds**
>   1 **pound skinless, boneless turkey breast, cut into ¼- by 2-inch strips**
>   1 **cup *each* regular-strength chicken broth and whipping cream**
>   2 **cups hot cooked rice**
> ½ **cup unsalted roasted cashews**

Heat oil in a 12- to 14-inch frying pan over medium-high heat. Add shallots and garlic and cook, stirring occasionally, until shallots are soft (about 6 minutes). Add ginger, chiles, coriander, cumin, turmeric, and fennel seeds. Cook, stirring, for 1 minute.

Add turkey. Cook, stirring often, until meat is no longer pink in center; cut to test (about 3 minutes). Remove turkey from pan and set aside.

Add broth and cream to pan; cook, stirring occasionally, until slightly thickened (about 5 minutes). Stir in turkey. Serve over rice; garnish with cashews. Makes 4 servings.

Per serving: 617 calories, 35 g protein, 39 g carbohydrates, 36 g fat, 15 g saturated fat, 137 mg cholesterol, 351 mg sodium

TURKEY SUMMER SQUASH STIR-FRY

Preparation time: About 15 minutes

Cooking time: About 8 minutes

To the cook, "stir-fry" is a synonym for "quick meal"—and this ginger-sparked dish is no exception. Succulent chunks of turkey are tossed together with tender-crisp squash strips in a tempting beer sauce.

>   **Cooking Sauce (recipe follows)**
>   1 **tablespoon *each* cornstarch and rice wine**
>   1 **pound skinless, boneless turkey breast, cut into ¾-inch cubes**
>   2 **tablespoons salad oil**
>   1 **clove garlic, minced or pressed**
>   1 **teaspoon grated fresh ginger**
>   4 **medium-size crookneck squash (about 1 lb. *total*), cut into short, thin strips**

Prepare Cooking Sauce; set aside. In a bowl, stir together cornstarch and wine; add turkey and stir to coat. Set aside.

Heat oil in a 12- to 14-inch frying pan over medium-high heat; add garlic and ginger and stir once. Add turkey and cook, stirring often, until no longer pink in center; cut to test (about 5 minutes). Remove turkey and set aside. Add squash and cook, stirring often, until tender-crisp to bite (about 2 minutes). Return turkey to pan, then stir in Cooking Sauce and cook, stirring, until sauce boils and thickens. Makes 4 servings.

COOKING SAUCE. In a small bowl, stir together 1½ tablespoons **cornstarch,** 1 teaspoon **sugar,** ½ cup **regular-strength chicken broth,** ¼ cup **beer,** and 1 tablespoon **rice wine.**

Per serving: 250 calories, 28 g protein, 12 g carbohydrates, 9 g fat, 1 g saturated fat, 70 mg cholesterol, 203 mg sodium

TURKEY CHILI

Preparation time: About 15 minutes

Cooking time: About 50 minutes

Chili fanatics may not even deign to call this "chili": after all, it contains beans and soy sauce, and there's not a scrap of beef to be found. Nonetheless, even the purists will probably be back for seconds! Serve with your favorite toppings.

- 2 tablespoons salad oil
- 1 medium-size onion, chopped
- 1 small green bell pepper, seeded and chopped
- 1 clove garlic, minced or pressed
- 1½ pounds skinless, boneless turkey breast, cut into bite-size chunks
- 1 small can (about 8 oz.) tomatoes, drained and chopped
- 2 cans (about 15 oz. *each*) kidney beans, drained
- 1 large can (15 oz.) tomato sauce
- 2 tablespoons soy sauce
- 1½ tablespoons chili powder
- ½ teaspoon *each* ground cumin, dry sage leaves, and dry thyme leaves
   Toppings (suggestions follow)

Heat oil in a 4- to 5-quart pan over medium-high heat; add onion, bell pepper, and garlic. Cook, stirring often, until onion is soft (about 7 minutes). Remove from pan and set aside.

Increase heat to high. Add half the turkey and cook, stirring often, until no longer pink in center; cut to test (about 5 minutes). Remove from pan; set aside. Repeat to cook remaining turkey.

Return onion mixture and all turkey to pan. Then add tomatoes, beans, tomato sauce, soy, chili powder, cumin, sage, and thyme. Bring to a boil; reduce heat, cover, and simmer until chili is thick and flavors are well blended (about 30 minutes; uncover for last 5 minutes).

Ladle hot chili into bowls; offer toppings to embellish individual servings. Makes 6 servings.

TOPPINGS. Offer **lime wedges**, sliced **green onions** (including tops), shredded **jack or Cheddar cheese**, and chopped **tomatoes.**

Per serving: 310 calories, 32 g protein, 29 g carbohydrates, 8 g fat, 1 g saturated fat, 70 mg cholesterol, 1,247 mg sodium

GRILLED TURKEY CHUNKS PICCATA

Preparation time: About 15 minutes

Marinating time: At least 30 minutes or up to 2 hours

Grilling time: About 15 minutes

Searching for simple summer fare? Try tender, caper-topped turkey chunks freshened with a lemon-pepper marinade. Grill zucchini halves alongside the skewered meat.

- 3 tablespoons capers with liquid
- ½ cup lemon juice
- 2 tablespoons olive oil
- ¼ teaspoon pepper
- 2 pounds skinless, boneless turkey breast, cut into 1-inch cubes
- 4 medium-size zucchini (about 1½ lbs. total)
   Lemon wedges

Drain caper liquid into a shallow dish; cover drained capers and refrigerate. Stir lemon juice, oil, and pepper into caper liquid. Add turkey and stir to coat. Cover and refrigerate for at least 30 minutes or up to 2 hours.

Drain turkey; reserve marinade. Thread turkey equally on 6 metal skewers. Cut each zucchini in half lengthwise; coat zucchini with marinade.

Place turkey and zucchini on a lightly greased grill 4 to 6 inches above a solid bed of medium coals. Cook, turning as needed and basting several times with marinade, until turkey is no longer pink in center; cut to test (about 15 minutes). Sprinkle with drained capers; offer lemon wedges to squeeze over meat. Makes 6 servings.

Per serving: 233 calories, 37 g protein, 5 g carbohydrates, 7 g fat, 1 g saturated fat, 94 mg cholesterol, 219 mg sodium

Hungry guests will greet dinner with glee when they see this hearty dish!
A savory tomato sauce, thick with big chunks of turkey, crowns squares of
cheese-topped polenta. Accompany our Broiled Turkey with Baked Polenta
(recipe on page 80) with an oregano-seasoned summer squash sauté.

Succulent Legs & Thighs

SKEWERED & STUFFED & WINED & MINTED &

STIR-FRIED & CRUMBED & CURRIED & GRILLED &

TOMATOED & MUSHROOMED & OVEN-FRIED &

OVEN-FRIED BUTTERMILK CHICKEN LEGS

Preparation time: About 10 minutes

Baking time: About 45 minutes

Shake a leg—or rather legs—and get this main course in the oven in minutes: simply toss chicken in a bag with a buttermilk-tangy crumb coating. Bake acorn squash and small russet potatoes alongside for an almost effortless dinner.

- ½ **cup fine dry bread crumbs**
- ¼ **cup dry buttermilk**
- ½ **teaspoon** *each* **dry thyme leaves and dry oregano leaves**
- 6 **whole chicken legs (about 3 lbs.** *total***)**
- 3 **tablespoons butter or margarine, melted**
  Salt and pepper

In a paper or plastic bag, combine crumbs, dry buttermilk, thyme, and oregano. Rinse chicken and shake off most of the moisture; then shake chicken in bag to coat evenly with crumb mixture.

Arrange chicken legs slightly apart in a greased shallow 10- by 15-inch baking pan. Drizzle with butter. Bake, uncovered, in a 400° oven until coating is brown and crisp and meat near thighbone is no longer pink; cut to test (about 45 minutes). Season to taste with salt and pepper. Makes 6 servings.

Per serving: 398 calories, 32 g protein, 7 g carbohydrates, 26 g fat, 9 g saturated fat, 154 mg cholesterol, 262 mg sodium

CRANBERRY CHICKEN

Preparation time: About 10 minutes

Baking time: About 1 hour

A sweet-tart cranberry glaze elevates easy baked chicken from ordinary to extra-special. And because the recipe works well with both fresh and frozen berries, you can enjoy it all year long. You might round out the meal with French fries and a tossed salad.

- 1 **tablespoon butter or margarine**
- 1 **small onion, chopped**
- 6 **whole chicken legs (about 3 lbs.** *total***), skinned if desired**
- ⅔ **cup catsup**
- ⅓ **cup firmly packed brown sugar**
- 1 **tablespoon cider vinegar**
- 1 **teaspoon dry mustard**
- 1½ **cups fresh or frozen cranberries**

Place butter in a shallow 10- by 15-inch baking pan; set pan in a 400° oven until butter is melted. Stir in onion. Bake, uncovered, until onion is pale gold (about 15 minutes), stirring occasionally. Meanwhile, rinse chicken and pat dry.

Push onion to one side of pan; arrange chicken in a single layer in pan (not on top of onion). Continue to bake, uncovered, for 25 more minutes; stir onion occasionally.

In a bowl, stir together catsup, sugar, vinegar, mustard, and cranberries. Spoon browned onions out

of pan and stir them into cranberry mixture; space chicken evenly in pan, then top evenly with cranberry mixture. Continue to bake until cranberry mixture is slightly caramelized and chicken meat near thighbone is no longer pink; cut to test (about 20 more minutes). Makes 6 servings.

Per serving: 422 calories, 31 g protein, 24 g carbohydrates, 22 g fat, 7 g saturated fat, 143 mg cholesterol, 472 mg sodium

BAKED CHICKEN WITH TOMATO-CHEESE PASTA

Preparation time: About 10 minutes

Cooking time: About 45 minutes

Company casserole or family feast? This meal fits either role. Top small pasta seashells with diced tomatoes and a luscious, creamy-rich blend of Neufchâtel cheese, butter, and Parmesan; offer basil-sprinkled baked chicken on top or alongside.

- 4 to 6 whole chicken legs (2 to 3 lbs. *total*)
- 8 ounces dry small shell-shaped or round pasta
- 1 tablespoon olive oil
- 1 large package (8 oz.) Neufchâtel or cream cheese, at room temperature
- ½ cup (¼ lb.) unsalted butter or margarine, at room temperature
- ⅓ cup grated Parmesan cheese
- 3 medium-size pear-shaped tomatoes (about 6 oz. *total*), chopped
- 1 tablespoon chopped fresh basil leaves or 1 teaspoon dry basil leaves
  Basil sprigs

Rinse chicken, pat dry, and arrange in a single layer in a shallow baking pan. Bake, uncovered, in a 400° oven for 35 minutes.

Meanwhile, cook pasta according to package directions just until tender to bite. Drain; place in a shallow 2- to 3-quart baking dish, lightly mix in oil, and set aside.

In a medium-size bowl, combine Neufchâtel cheese, butter, and ¼ cup of the Parmesan cheese; beat with an electric mixer until well blended. Mound cheese mixture in center of pasta; sprinkle tomatoes over cheese mixture.

When chicken has baked for 35 minutes, place cheese-topped pasta in oven. Bake, uncovered, until pasta is hot in center and meat near chicken thighbone is no longer pink; cut to test (about 10 minutes). Arrange chicken over pasta around edge of baking dish. Sprinkle with chopped basil and remaining Parmesan cheese; garnish with basil sprigs. Makes 4 to 6 servings.

Per serving: 763 calories, 42 g protein, 37 g carbohydrates, 49 g fat, 24 g saturated fat, 191 mg cholesterol, 385 mg sodium

■ *Pictured on page 2*

SAUTÉED CHICKEN WITH CORINTH GRAPES

Preparation time: About 5 minutes

Cooking time: About 37 minutes

Black Corinth grapes, frequently marketed as "champagne grapes," add an elegant touch to this dinner-for-two version of classic chicken Véronique. You simmer whole chicken legs in a sweet white wine–cream sauce, then add clusters of grapes to the cooking pan.

You'll find Black Corinth grapes in markets and produce shops from mid-July to mid-October.

- 2 whole chicken legs (about 1 lb. *total*)
- 1 tablespoon butter or margarine
- 1 tablespoon olive oil
- ½ cup late-harvest sweet white wine, such as Johannisberg Riesling
- ½ cup whipping cream
- 2 clusters Black Corinth grapes (*each* about 1½ inches wide and 4 inches long)
  Salt and pepper

Rinse chicken and pat dry. Melt butter in oil in a 10- to 12-inch frying pan over medium-high heat. Add chicken and cook, turning as needed, until browned on both sides (about 6 minutes). Reduce heat to medium-low, cover, and continue to cook until meat near thighbone is no longer pink; cut to test (about 25 more minutes). Transfer chicken to dinner plates; keep warm.

Pour off and discard fat from pan, then pour in wine and boil over high heat until reduced to 2 tablespoons (about 3 minutes). Stir in cream. Place grapes in pan and reduce heat to medium; cook, turning clusters several times, until grapes are slightly softened and sauce is slightly thicker (about 3 minutes).

Place grapes alongside chicken, then pour sauce over both. Season to taste with salt and pepper. Makes 2 servings.

Per serving: 601 calories, 31 g protein, 17 g carbohydrates, 46 g fat, 20 g saturated fat, 185 mg cholesterol, 181 mg sodium

■ *Pictured on front cover*

CHICKEN WITH OLIVES & PINE NUTS

Preparation time: About 10 minutes

Cooking time: About 45 minutes

Fit for a festival! The sunny Mediterranean flavor of chicken simmered with fresh sage and salty green olives should cheer up any crowd. Toasted pine nuts accent the dish.

- ⅔ **cup pine nuts**
- 8 *each* **chicken drumsticks and thighs (about 4 lbs. *total*), skinned**
- 1 **tablespoon butter or margarine**
- 1 **tablespoon olive oil**
- 2 **cups drained unpitted Spanish-style olives**
- 5 **fresh sage leaves or 1 teaspoon dry sage leaves**
- ¼ **cup water**
  Fresh sage leaves (optional)

Toast pine nuts in a 12- to 14-inch frying pan over medium-low heat until golden brown (about 7 minutes), shaking pan often. Remove nuts from pan and set aside.

Rinse chicken and pat dry. Melt butter in oil in pan over medium-high heat. Add chicken, a portion at a time; cook, turning as needed, until browned on all sides (about 6 minutes).

Pour off and discard fat from pan, then return pine nuts and all chicken (and any accumulated juices) to pan. Add olives, the 5 sage leaves (or all the dry sage), and water. Bring to a simmer. Then reduce heat to medium-low, cover, and simmer until meat near thighbone is no longer pink; cut to test (about 25 minutes).

Transfer chicken mixture to a platter; garnish with sage leaves, if desired. Makes 8 servings.

Per serving: 271 calories, 29 g protein, 2 g carbohydrates, 17 g fat, 3 g saturated fat, 105 mg cholesterol, 935 mg sodium

■ *Pictured on facing page*

MUSTARD CHICKEN & PASTA

Preparation time: About 10 minutes

Cooking time: About 1 hour

The Dijon mustard sauce alone is enough to make this meal a hit. Half-and-half and a rich-tasting broth from simmered chicken contribute to the wonderful flavor. You can serve the chicken and sauce over any pasta shapes; try tricolor *radiatore* for an unusual touch.

- 6 **whole chicken legs (about 3 lbs. *total*)**
- 2 **cups regular-strength chicken broth**
- ¼ **cup butter or margarine**
- ¼ **cup all-purpose flour**
- 1 **cup half-and-half or milk**
- 2 **tablespoons Dijon mustard**
- ½ **teaspoon dry thyme leaves**
  Salt and pepper
- 12 **ounces dry pasta shapes, such as radiatore**
- ¼ **cup finely chopped parsley**
  Parsley sprigs

Rinse chicken and pat dry; then place in a wide, heavy 4- to 5-quart pan. Add broth and bring to a boil over medium-high heat. Reduce heat, cover,

and simmer for 30 minutes. Lift out chicken and set aside. Skim and discard fat from broth, then measure out 1¾ cups broth. Reserve remaining broth for other uses.

In pan used to cook chicken, melt butter over medium heat. Blend in flour and cook, stirring, until bubbly. Remove from heat; gradually stir in the 1¾ cups broth, then half-and-half, until blended. Return to heat and continue to cook, stirring, until mixture boils and thickens. Blend in mustard and thyme; season to taste with salt and pepper.

Remove and discard skin from chicken. Place chicken in sauce and simmer, uncovered, until meat near thighbone is no longer pink; cut to test (about 15 minutes).

Meanwhile, cook pasta according to package directions just until tender to bite. Drain well and mound in center of a serving dish or deep platter.

Lift chicken from sauce and arrange around edge of platter. Stir chopped parsley into sauce; pour sauce over pasta and chicken. Garnish with parsley sprigs. Makes 6 servings.

Per serving: 517 calories, 36 g protein, 49 g carbohydrates, 19 g fat, 9 g saturated fat, 139 mg cholesterol, 669 mg sodium

Spoil your family with a special meal: Mustard Chicken & Pasta
(recipe on facing page). Succulent chicken legs and tricolor pasta shapes are
cloaked in a rich, parsley-flecked mustard cream sauce. Alongside, serve
baby carrots tossed with butter and fresh thyme.

TANDOORI BARBECUED CHICKEN

Preparation time: About 15 minutes, plus 30 minutes to heat coals

Marinating time: At least 1 hour or up to 1 day

Grilling time: About 40 minutes

Tandoori chicken translates beautifully to your back-yard barbecue. Marinate whole legs in a tart blend of yogurt, lime, and spices, then grill them slowly over indirect heat. Serve with rice pilaf and sliced tomatoes.

 2 tablespoons white wine vinegar
 ¼ cup lime juice
 ½ teaspoon *each* crushed dried hot red chiles and cumin seeds
 1 teaspoon ground turmeric
1½ teaspoons paprika
 ¼ cup chopped fresh cilantro (coriander)
 3 cloves garlic
 1 tablespoon minced fresh ginger
 ¼ cup chopped parsley
 1 cup plain low-fat yogurt
 6 to 8 whole chicken legs (3 to 4 lbs. *total*)

In a blender or food processor, combine vinegar, lime juice, chiles, cumin seeds, turmeric, paprika, cilantro, garlic, ginger, and parsley. Whirl until smoothly puréed. Turn mixture into a large bowl, add yogurt, and mix well.

Rinse chicken and pat dry. Make a cut through to thigh and drumstick bones along entire length of each leg. Add chicken to yogurt mixture; turn to coat well. Cover and refrigerate for at least 1 hour or up to 1 day.

Prepare a covered barbecue for grilling by indirect heat as directed for Barbecued Turkey on page 22.

Drain chicken; reserve yogurt marinade. Then arrange chicken on lightly greased grill directly above drip pan. Cover barbecue and adjust dampers as necessary to maintain an even heat. Cook chicken, basting often with marinade, until meat near thighbone is no longer pink; cut to test (about 40 minutes). Makes 6 to 8 servings.

Per serving: 275 calories, 30 g protein, 2 g carbohydrates, 15 g fat, 4 g saturated fat, 104 mg cholesterol, 110 mg sodium

CURRY CHICKEN WITH CURRANTS

Preparation time: About 10 minutes

Cooking time: About 40 minutes

This uncomplicated curry offers proof positive that a minimum of ingredients can yield maximum flavor. Chicken thighs, chopped onion and bell pepper, and currants simmer together in a tomato-based sauce; salted almonds add a crunchy accent.

 3 pounds chicken thighs
   About ¾ cup all-purpose flour
 2 tablespoons salad oil
 1 large onion, chopped
 1 large green bell pepper (about 6 oz.), seeded and chopped
 2 cloves garlic, minced or pressed
 1 tablespoon curry powder
 1 can (14½ oz.) tomatoes
 1 teaspoon liquid hot pepper seasoning
 ½ cup dried currants
   Salt
 ½ cup chopped salted roasted almonds

Rinse chicken and pat dry. Roll in flour to coat; shake off excess.

Heat oil in a 12- to 14-inch frying pan over medium-high heat. Add chicken, a portion at a time; cook, turning as needed, until browned on all sides (about 6 minutes). Remove from pan and set aside. Add onion, bell pepper, garlic, and curry powder; reduce heat to low and cook, stirrring, until vegetables are limp (about 7 minutes).

Add tomatoes (break up with a spoon) and their liquid, hot pepper seasoning, and currants; then add chicken and any accumulated juices. Bring to a boil. Reduce heat, cover, and simmer until meat near bone is no longer pink; cut to test (about 20 minutes). Skim and discard fat from sauce; season to taste with salt. Spoon chicken and sauce into a serving dish and garnish with almonds. Makes 6 servings.

Per serving: 624 calories, 37 g protein, 30 g carbohydrates, 40 g fat, 9 mg saturated fat, 151 mg cholesterol, 375 mg sodium

BRAISED TERIYAKI CHICKEN

Preparation time: About 10 minutes

Cooking time: About 45 minutes

This version of teriyaki chicken is simmered, not grilled, so the meat is extra-juicy. The sauce features the familiar soy and garlic—but you'll also taste onion, red bell pepper, white wine (not the usual sherry), and even sweet raisins.

    8 chicken thighs (about 2 lbs. *total*), skinned
    1 tablespoon butter or margarine
    1 tablespoon olive oil or salad oil
    1 medium-size onion, chopped
    1 medium-size red bell pepper, seeded and chopped
    2 cloves garlic, minced or pressed
    2 small dried hot red chiles
    ¾ cup dry white wine
    ¼ cup soy sauce
    ½ cup raisins
       Cilantro (coriander) sprigs

Rinse chicken and pat dry. Melt butter in oil in a 10- to 12-inch frying pan over medium-high heat. Add chicken, a portion at a time; cook, turning as needed, until browned on all sides (about 6 minutes). Remove from pan and set aside.

Add onion, bell pepper, and garlic to pan; cook, stirring often, until onion is soft (about 7 minutes). Add chiles, wine, and soy; stir to blend. Push vegetables to sides of pan. Arrange chicken in center of pan; add any accumulated juices.

Bring to a boil over high heat. Then reduce heat, cover, and simmer until meat near bone is no longer pink; cut to test (about 20 minutes).

With a slotted spoon, transfer chicken and vegetables to a platter and keep warm. Skim and discard fat from sauce; stir in raisins, then boil sauce over high heat until reduced to about ½ cup (about 5 minutes). Remove and discard chiles, if desired. Pour sauce over chicken and garnish with cilantro. Makes 4 servings.

Per serving: 291 calories, 28 g protein, 20 g carbohydrates, 12 g fat, 4 g saturated fat, 115 mg cholesterol, 1,175 mg sodium

ESCABÈCHE OF CHICKEN

Preparation time: About 10 minutes

Cooking time: About 45 minutes

Serve up a taste of Spain with this entrée! Small whole onions and succulent chicken thighs simmer in a spicy red wine sauce made piquant with a splash of sherry vinegar.

    8 chicken thighs (about 2 lbs. *total*), skinned
    2 tablespoons olive oil
       Escabèche Sauce with Onions (recipe follows)
       Salt

Rinse chicken and pat dry. Heat oil in a 10- to 12-inch frying pan over medium-high heat. Add chicken, a portion at a time; cook, turning as needed, until browned on all sides (about 6 minutes). Remove from pan and set aside.

Use pan (with any remaining oil and chicken drippings in it) to prepare Escabèche Sauce with Onions. Add chicken and any accumulated juices to sauce; bring to a boil over high heat. Then reduce heat, cover,

and simmer until meat near bone is no longer pink; cut to test (about 20 minutes).

With a slotted spoon, transfer chicken and whole onions to a platter; keep warm. Skim and discard fat from sauce; then boil sauce over high heat until reduced to 1 cup (about 3 minutes). If desired, remove and discard bay leaf, chiles, and cinnamon stick. Pour sauce over chicken. Season to taste with salt. Makes 4 servings.

ESCABÈCHE SAUCE WITH ONIONS. To pan used to brown chicken, add 2 or 3 cloves **garlic,** minced; 1 small **onion,** chopped; 1 **dry bay leaf;** 3 **small dried hot red chiles;** 6 **dry juniper berries;** 1 **cinnamon stick** (about 3 inches long); and ½ teaspoon *each* **ground coriander** and **dry thyme leaves.** Cook over medium heat, stirring often, until onion is soft (about 7 minutes). Then stir in 1 tablespoon **tomato paste,** ⅔ cup **dry red wine,** ⅓ cup **regular-strength chicken broth,** ¼ cup **sherry vinegar** or red wine vinegar, and 1 package (10 oz.) **frozen small whole onions.** Stir to mix well.

Per serving: 287 calories, 27 g protein, 11 g carbohydrates, 12 g fat, 2 g saturated fat, 107 mg cholesterol, 235 mg sodium

There's something for everyone in our Brown Rice Paella (recipe on facing page). Chicken thighs, chorizo, pork, shrimp, and even oysters mingle in this hearty company entrée. Offer lots of crunchy-crusted bread to soak up the saffron-flavored broth.

■ Pictured on facing page

BROWN RICE PAELLA

Preparation time: About 15 minutes

Cooking time: About 2 hours

Thinking of a special dinner? Think paella: Saffron-scented rice studded with chicken, sausage, and shellfish. Our version calls for brown rice, adds pork shoulder, and omits the usual mussels or clams, but your tastebuds won't object to the twist on tradition.

- 2 to 3 tablespoons olive oil
- 8 small onions (*each* about 1 inch in diameter), quartered
- 1 pound boneless pork shoulder or butt (trimmed of excess fat), cut into ½-inch cubes
- 8 chicken thighs (about 2 lbs. *total*), skinned
- 12 ounces chorizo sausages, casings removed
- 2 cups long-grain brown rice
- ¹⁄₁₆ teaspoon powdered saffron
- 4 cups regular-strength chicken broth, heated
- 1 can (14½ oz.) stewed tomatoes
- 1 jar (4 oz.) sliced pimentos, drained
- ½ cup chopped parsley
- 1 pound tiny cooked and shelled shrimp
- 1 jar (10 oz.) small Pacific oysters (optional)

Heat 2 tablespoons of the oil in a 6- to 8-quart pan over medium heat. Add onions; cook, stirring often, until lightly browned (about 5 minutes). Remove from pan and set aside. Add pork to pan; cook, stirring often, until browned (about 20 minutes). Remove from pan and set aside.

Rinse chicken; pat dry. Add to pan, a portion at a time; cook, turning as needed, until browned on all sides (about 8 minutes), adding more oil if needed to prevent sticking. Remove from pan; set aside. Add chorizo to pan and crumble with a spoon; cook, stirring often, until browned (about 15 minutes). Spoon off and discard all but 3 tablespoons of the drippings. Add rice to pan; stir until opaque (about 8 minutes).

Moisten saffron with 2 tablespoons of the hot broth. Add saffron mixture to pan along with remaining broth, onions, and pork; stir well. Bring to a boil over high heat; reduce heat, cover, and simmer for 20 minutes. Stir in tomatoes, then add chicken and any accumulated juices. Cover and continue to simmer until rice is tender to bite and chicken meat near bone is no longer pink; cut to test (about 20 more minutes).

Add pimentos, parsley, shrimp, and (if desired) oysters and their liquid. Stir gently to mix; cover. Cook over lowest heat for 5 minutes. Makes 8 servings.

Per serving: 588 calories, 47 g protein, 43 g carbohydrates, 24 g fat, 7 g saturated fat, 230 mg cholesterol, 1,026 mg sodium

CHICKEN WITH BARLEY & PECANS

Preparation time: About 10 minutes

Cooking time: About 1 hour and 20 minutes

This one-dish dinner qualifies as true comfort food—with a touch of style. Toasted pecans top a soothing blend of barley, chicken, and mushrooms in broth.

- 8 chicken thighs (about 2 lbs. *total*), skinned
- 3 tablespoons olive oil or salad oil
- ½ cup pecan halves
- 1 large onion, chopped
- 1 pound mushrooms, thinly sliced
- 1 cup pearl barley
- 2 cloves garlic, minced or pressed
- 3 cups regular-strength chicken broth
- 2 tablespoons minced parsley

Rinse chicken, pat dry, and set aside. Heat 1 tablespoon of the oil in a 10- to 12-inch frying pan over medium-low heat. Add pecans and cook, stirring, until nuts have a toasted flavor and are golden inside; break a nut to test (about 7 minutes). Remove from pan with a slotted spoon and set aside.

Increase heat to medium-high; heat 1 tablespoon more oil in pan. Add chicken, a portion at a time; cook, turning as needed, until browned on all sides (about 6 minutes). Remove from pan and set aside.

Heat remaining 1 tablespoon oil in pan. Add onion and mushrooms; cook, stirring often, until onion is soft (about 7 minutes). Add barley and garlic; cook, stirring, until barley starts to turn golden (about 2 minutes). Add broth; bring to a boil. Reduce heat, cover, and simmer for 20 minutes. Add chicken and any accumulated juices; cover. Continue to simmer until barley is tender to bite and chicken meat near bone is no longer pink; cut to test (about 30 more minutes). Top with pecans and parsley. Makes 4 servings.

Per serving: 575 calories, 37 g protein, 51 g carbohydrates, 26 g fat, 4 g saturated fat, 107 mg cholesterol, 862 mg sodium

OVEN-SMOKED POULTRY

When you crave succulent hickory-scented chicken but don't feel like firing up the barbecue, use the oven instead. "Oven-smoking" simply takes advantage of liquid smoke, a pale chestnut-colored liquid sold in supermarkets alongside Worcestershire and other seasoning sauces. Though it doesn't preserve food as true smoking does, liquid smoke imparts the same savory flavor.

Liquid smoke really is made from smoke. The smoke from burning wood is caught in tubes, where it cools and condenses; the resulting liquid is then filtered and bottled. Hickory wood is the most common source of liquid smoke, but you may find other "flavors"—mesquite, for example—in specialty markets.

Oven-smoking is a simple process. Choose a tight-lidded pan and a rack that will fit inside it; pour a few tablespoons of liquid smoke into the pan, place the poultry of your choice on the rack, and cook. The food essentially steams as it bakes, absorbing flavor as the liquid smoke evaporates. To adjust the "smokiness" of your poultry, vary the amount of liquid smoke used, keeping in mind that the flavor grows stronger as the food cools. Because liquid smoke's aroma can fill your kitchen, you may prefer to do your oven-smoking the day before serving—you want your family and guests to be enticed by the fragrance, not knocked out cold. Oven-smoked poultry keeps in the refrigerator for 2 days; be sure to wrap it securely, so it won't flavor the foods stored around it.

The following instructions and chart present the basics of oven-smoking. We also suggest a tempting use for smoked chicken breasts: a luncheon salad of chicken, toasted pecans, and crisp greens with a sweet-tangy orange vinaigrette.

Basic directions for oven-smoking: Pour 3 tablespoons **liquid smoke** into a 5- to 6-quart pan. Set a perforated or wire rack in pan. Arrange **poultry** of your choice (see chart at left below) in a single layer on rack; tightly cover pan. Bake in a 350° oven until poultry tests done (see chart for times and tests). If made ahead, let cool; then cover and refrigerate for up to 2 days.

SMOKED CHICKEN SALAD

Preparation time: About 40 minutes, plus 2 hours to chill chicken

Cooking time: About 7 minutes

> Orange Vinaigrette (recipe follows)
> 1 tablespoon butter or margarine
> ¾ cup pecan halves
> 6 cups bite-size pieces washed, crisped mixed salad greens, such as butter lettuce, romaine lettuce, and watercress
> 4 smoked chicken breast halves (see chart at left below), chilled

Prepare Orange Vinaigrette; set aside. Melt butter in a 10- to 12-inch frying pan over medium-low heat. Add pecans and cook, stirring occasionally, until nuts have a toasted flavor and are golden inside; break a nut to test (about 7 minutes). Drain on paper towels. Arrange salad greens equally on 4 dinner plates; sprinkle evenly with pecans.

Cut each breast half into ¼-inch-thick slanting slices. On each plate, arrange one sliced breast half alongside greens, fanning out slices. Spoon Orange Vinaigrette over greens and chicken. Makes 4 servings.

ORANGE VINAIGRETTE. In a bowl, mix ¼ cup **orange juice,** 2 tablespoons *each* **white wine vinegar** and **salad oil,** 1 tablespoon thinly slivered or shredded **orange peel,** 2 teaspoons *each* **honey** and **Dijon mustard,** and ½ teaspoon coarsely ground **pepper.**

Per serving: 372 calories, 36 g protein, 10 g carbohydrates, 21 g fat, 4 g saturated fat, 93 mg cholesterol, 211 mg sodium

Poultry	Maximum amount or size	Cooking time
Skinless, boneless chicken breast halves	4 breast halves (about 4 oz. each)	About 20 minutes*
Whole chicken legs	4 legs (about 2 lbs. total)	About 40 minutes**
Whole chicken	3 to 3½ pounds	About 1¼ hours**
Cornish game hens	2 (2½ lbs. total)	About 1 hour**

*Done when meat in thickest part is no longer pink; cut to test.
**Done when meat near thighbone is no longer pink; cut to test.

GRILLED ASIAN CHICKEN

Preparation time: About 15 minutes

Marinating time: At least 4 hours or up to 1 day

Grilling time: About 30 minutes

A paste of garlic, cilantro, and black peppercorns packs a powerful punch. Slipped beneath the skin of chicken thighs before grilling, it flavors the meat more thoroughly than any baste could.

- 8 **chicken thighs (about 2 lbs. *total*)**
- 6 **cloves garlic**
- ½ **cup fresh cilantro (coriander) leaves**
- 2 **teaspoons whole black peppercorns**
- 2 **teaspoons soy sauce**
- 1 **teaspoon sugar**
- 5 **tablespoons salad oil**
- 1 **tablespoon wine vinegar**

Rinse chicken, pat dry, and set aside.

In a blender or food processor, whirl garlic, cilantro, and peppercorns until finely chopped. Add soy, sugar, and ¼ cup of the oil; whirl to form a paste. Measure out 1½ tablespoons of the paste; cover and refrigerate. Rub remaining paste evenly all over chicken, slipping some under skin. Cover and refrigerate for at least 4 hours or up to 1 day.

Place chicken, skin side up, on a lightly greased grill 4 to 6 inches above a solid bed of medium coals. Cook, turning often, until meat near bone is no longer pink; cut to test (about 30 minutes). Mix reserved paste, vinegar, and remaining 1 tablespoon oil; spoon over chicken. Makes 4 servings.

Per serving: 401 calories, 30 g protein, 2 g carbohydrates, 30 g fat, 7 g saturated fat, 109 mg cholesterol, 214 mg sodium

APPLE COUNTRY CHICKEN

Preparation time: About 10 minutes

Cooking time: About 40 minutes

Curried chicken goes country when Golden Delicious apples and cider are added to the cooking pan. This dish can be ready to serve in under an hour; top it with spoonfuls of tart yogurt, if you like.

- 3 **pounds chicken thighs, skinned**
- 1½ **teaspoons curry powder**
- 2 **large Golden Delicious apples, cored and chopped**
- 1 **large onion, chopped**
- 1 **cup cider or apple juice**
- 1 **cup regular-strength chicken broth**
- 1 **tablespoon lemon juice**
- 4 **ounces mushrooms, sliced**
- 1 **tablespoon all-purpose flour**
- 2 **tablespoons sliced green onion (including top)**
- 1 **cup plain yogurt (optional)**

Rinse chicken, pat dry, and set aside.

Place curry powder in a 12- to 14-inch frying pan or 5- to 6-quart pan; stir over medium heat until slightly darker in color (about 4 minutes). Add apples, chopped onion, cider, ½ cup of the broth, lemon juice, and mushrooms; bring to a boil over high heat. Add chicken, reduce heat, cover, and simmer until meat near bone is no longer pink; cut to test (about 30 minutes). With a slotted spoon, transfer chicken to a platter. Keep warm.

Skim and discard fat from chicken cooking liquid. Blend flour and remaining ½ cup broth; add to pan. Boil over high heat, stirring often, until reduced to 3 cups. Pour sauce over chicken. Garnish with green onion; add yogurt to taste, if desired. Makes 6 servings.

Per serving: 233 calories, 27 g protein, 18 g carbohydrates, 6 g fat, 1 g saturated fat, 107 mg cholesterol, 279 mg sodium

CURRIED TURKEY DRUMSTICKS

Preparation time: About 15 minutes

Grilling time: About 55 minutes

No arguments over who gets the drumsticks this time — there's one for every member of the family. Flavor the turkey with a ginger-sparked curry butter before grilling; offer crunchy peanut sauce at the table.

- ¼ **cup butter or margarine, at room temperature**
- 4 **teaspoons curry powder**
- ¼ **teaspoon** *each* **ground ginger and ground cloves**
  Dash of pepper
- 4 **turkey drumsticks (about 1¼ lbs.** *each***)**
- ¼ **cup butter or margarine, melted**
  Peanut-Chile Sauce (recipe follows)

In a small bowl, blend room-temperature butter, curry powder, ginger, cloves, and pepper. Set aside.

Rinse turkey and pat dry. Carefully peel back skin on each drumstick and spread butter mixture evenly over meat. Pull skin back into place and secure with small metal skewers.

Place drumsticks on a lightly greased grill 4 to 6 inches above a solid bed of medium coals. Cover barbecue and adjust dampers (or cover with a tent of heavy-duty foil). Cook, turning as needed to cook evenly and basting often with melted butter, until meat near bone is no longer pink; cut to test (about 55 minutes).

Meanwhile, prepare Peanut-Chile Sauce. Pass sauce at the table to spoon over individual servings. Makes 4 servings.

Per serving without sauce: 794 calories, 79 g protein, 1 g carbohydrates, 51 g fat, 23 g saturated fat, 300 mg cholesterol, 451 mg sodium

PEANUT-CHILE SAUCE. In a small bowl, stir together ½ cup *each* **apple juice** and **crunchy peanut butter;** then stir in 1 teaspoon **crushed dried hot red chiles.** Makes about 1 cup.

Per tablespoon: 51 calories, 2 g protein, 3 g carbohydrates, 4 g fat, 1 g saturated fat, 0 mg cholesterol, 39 mg sodium

STUFFED TURKEY THIGHS

Preparation time: About 15 minutes

Baking time: About 1 hour

For holiday flavor without the fuss, bake boned turkey thighs stuffed with a savory celery and onion dressing. The casually festive entrée takes only about an hour to cook.

- 2 **turkey thighs (about 2 lbs.** *each***), boned**
- 2 **cups coarsely crushed packaged stuffing mix**
- ½ **cup finely chopped celery**
- 3 **tablespoons** *each* **chopped parsley and thinly sliced green onions (including tops)**
- ¼ **cup butter or margarine, melted**
- ½ **teaspoon poultry seasoning**
- ½ **cup regular-strength chicken broth**

Rinse turkey and pat dry; set aside.

In a large bowl, combine stuffing mix, celery, parsley, onions, butter, poultry seasoning, and broth.

To stuff turkey thighs, place them, skin side down, on a flat surface. Spoon about ¼ cup of the stuffing in center of each thigh where bone was removed. Bring meat up over stuffing and secure skin with metal skewers along 2 sides. Tuck more stuffing into open end; then secure skin across it with another skewer, completely enclosing meat and stuffing in a neat bundle. Wrap any remaining stuffing in foil.

Place turkey and foil-wrapped stuffing on a baking sheet. Bake, uncovered, in a 350° oven until meat in thickest part is no longer pink; cut to test (about 1 hour). To serve, remove skewers from turkey and cut each thigh crosswise into thick slices. Transfer extra stuffing from foil to a small bowl and serve alongside turkey. Makes 6 servings.

Per serving: 332 calories, 27 g protein, 18 g carbohydrates, 17 g fat, 7 g saturated fat, 107 mg cholesterol, 569 mg sodium

*Serve a spicy, easy-to-make peanut sauce over Curried Turkey
Drumsticks (recipe on facing page) at your next patio party. Cool tabbouli
and grilled pineapple slices and red bell pepper halves complete a
casual, colorful menu.*

■ *Pictured on page 66*

BROILED TURKEY WITH BAKED POLENTA

Preparation time: About 15 minutes

Broiling time: About 25 minutes

Baking time: About 50 minutes

A cool autumn day calls for a warm, colorful supper. Try bite-size pieces of broiled turkey thigh in a bright tomato and bell pepper sauce, served over crunchy, cheese-topped polenta.

2 pounds turkey thighs

1 onion, finely chopped

1 green bell pepper, seeded and chopped

1 can (14½ oz.) stewed tomatoes

1 can (8 oz.) tomato sauce

½ cup dry white wine

1 teaspoon *each* dry oregano leaves and dry basil leaves

5 cups regular-strength chicken broth

1½ cups polenta or yellow cornmeal

¼ cup butter or margarine, diced

½ cup grated Parmesan cheese

Rinse turkey and pat dry. Then arrange, skin side down, in a 9- by 13-inch baking pan. Broil about 4 inches below heat, turning once, until meat near bone is no longer pink; cut to test (about 25 minutes). Remove turkey from pan and set aside. To pan, add onion, bell pepper, tomatoes, tomato sauce, wine, oregano, and basil; mix well.

In a greased 9-inch-square baking pan, stir together broth, polenta, and butter.

Bake vegetable mixture and polenta, uncovered, in a 350° oven, stirring vegetables occasionally, until vegetables are very soft and have formed a thick sauce, and almost all polenta liquid has been absorbed (about 45 minutes).

Remove and discard skin and bones from turkey; cut meat into bite-size pieces. Stir meat into vegetable sauce; sprinkle cheese over polenta. Continue to bake, uncovered, until all polenta liquid has been absorbed (about 5 more minutes). Serve turkey and sauce over portions of polenta. Makes 6 servings.

Per serving: 446 calories, 29 g protein, 37 g carbohydrates, 20 g fat, 9 g saturated fat, 88 mg cholesterol, 1,484 mg sodium

SICHUAN TURKEY THIGH SCALOPPINE

Preparation time: About 15 minutes

Cooking time: About 15 minutes

If you think scaloppine always means veal and Italian flavors, you'll find this recipe unusual all the way around. The meat is pounded turkey thigh; the seasonings of garlic, fresh ginger, and Sichuan chili are Asian. You might serve the spicy sautéed slices with steamed rice and bok choy.

2½ pounds turkey thighs

3 tablespoons soy sauce

2 tablespoons Sichuan chili sauce or Chinese hot bean paste (or use pepper to taste)

About 3 tablespoons olive oil or salad oil

2 tablespoons minced shallots

1 tablespoon *each* minced garlic and minced fresh ginger

⅓ cup water

Pull off and discard turkey skin. Rinse turkey and pat dry; then place, skin side down, on a flat surface and find the thick bone with your fingers. Run a sharp knife along bone to cut meat free in a large, neat piece; lift bone with your other hand as you

cut. Discard bone. Cut meat into 6 equal-size pieces; lay any small scraps of meat in center of big pieces.

Place each turkey piece between 2 sheets of plastic wrap; pound with a flat-surfaced mallet to a thickness of about ¼ inch.

Mix soy and chili sauce; rub on both sides of turkey pieces (keep small scraps of meat in place on larger pieces). Set aside.

Heat 1 tablespoon of the oil in a 10- to 12-inch frying pan over medium-high heat. Add shallots, garlic, and ginger; cook, stirring, just until shallots are golden (about 3 minutes). Remove from pan with a slotted spoon and set aside. Heat 1 tablespoon more oil in pan; add turkey in a single layer (do not crowd pan). Cook until edges of turkey pieces turn white (about 2 minutes). Then turn and cook until meat is no longer pink in center; cut to test (about 2 minutes). Transfer cooked turkey to a platter and keep warm. Repeat to cook remaining turkey, adding more oil as necessary to prevent sticking.

Add water and shallot mixture to pan; stir to scrape up browned bits. Heat through, then pour over turkey. Makes 4 to 6 servings.

Per serving: 251 calories, 27 g protein, 4 g carbohydrates, 13 g fat, 3 g saturated fat, 97 mg cholesterol, 813 mg sodium

STIR-FRIED TURKEY SALAD

Preparation time: About 25 minutes

Cooking time: About 7 minutes

Stir-fried bacon slivers and turkey strips warm up this main-course salad. Pour the meat over tomato, avocado, and crisp butter lettuce, then toss with an assertive mustard dressing. Hot, crusty bread completes a hearty meal-in-minutes.

  2 **pounds turkey thighs**

 12 **cups bite-size pieces washed, crisped butter lettuce**

  1 **large tomato, cut into wedges**

  1 **large avocado, pitted, peeled, and sliced**

  ¼ **cup thinly sliced green onions (including tops)**

     Mustard Dressing (recipe follows)

  4 **slices bacon, cut into thin slivers**

  ¼ **cup grated Parmesan cheese**

Skin and bone turkey as directed for Sichuan Turkey Thigh Scaloppine (page 80). Cut meat into ¼- by 2-inch julienne strips and set aside.

Arrange lettuce, tomato, avocado, and onions in a large salad bowl. Set aside. Prepare Mustard Dressing; set aside.

Cook bacon in a wok or 12- to 14-inch frying pan over medium-high heat until crisp (about 4 minutes). With a slotted spoon, remove bacon from pan and set aside. Pour off and discard all but 1 tablespoon of the drippings.

Increase heat to high. Add turkey to drippings in pan and cook, stirring often, until lightly browned on outside and no longer pink in center; cut to test (about 3 minutes). Pour turkey and pan juices over salad; then pour dressing over salad. Add cheese and bacon; toss to mix. Makes 4 to 6 servings.

MUSTARD DRESSING. In a small bowl, stir together ¼ cup **salad oil**, 3 tablespoons *each* **mayonnaise** and **red wine vinegar**, 1 tablespoon **Dijon mustard**, and 1 teaspoon **dry thyme leaves**.

Per serving: 449 calories, 26 g protein, 8 g carbohydrates, 35 g fat, 7 g saturated fat, 92 mg cholesterol, 398 mg sodium

SKEWERED TURKEY

Preparation time: About 15 minutes

Marinating time: At least 1 hour or up to 1 day

Grilling time: About 15 minutes

Guests will think they're dining on lamb when you serve turkey flavored by a mint jelly marinade. The meat needs to soak for at least an hour, but if you like, you can marinate it up to a full day before grilling. Serve the sizzling-hot skewers with fluffy rice.

  2 **pounds turkey thighs**

  ¼ **cup** *each* **salad oil and dry white wine**

  ¼ **cup mint jelly, melted**

  ¼ **teaspoon grated lime peel**

  1 **tablespoon lime juice**

  ⅛ **teaspoon pepper**

     Hot cooked rice

Skin and bone turkey as directed for Sichuan Turkey Thigh Scaloppine (page 80); cut meat into 1-inch chunks.

In a bowl, stir together oil, wine, jelly, lime peel, lime juice, and pepper. Then add turkey and stir to coat. Cover and refrigerate for at least 1 hour or up to 1 day, stirring several times.

Drain turkey; reserve marinade. Thread meat equally on 4 metal skewers. Place skewers on a lightly greased grill 4 to 6 inches above a solid bed of medium coals. Cook, turning as needed and basting several times with marinade, until turkey is well browned on outside and no longer pink in center; cut to test (about 15 minutes).

To serve, mound rice on a platter; top with skewered turkey. Makes 4 servings.

Per serving: 249 calories, 26 g protein, 7 g carbohydrates, 12 g fat, 3 g saturated fat, 97 mg cholesterol, 106 mg sodium

Big appetites call for plates piled high with mashed potatoes, cole slaw, and Oven-fried Turkey Wings (recipe on page 89). A crisp cornmeal crust seasoned with marjoram and paprika makes this meaty, down-home main course extra satisfying.

Saucy Wings & Drummettes

CRUSTED & SPICED & CHILIED & GLAZED &

MARINATED & DIPPED & BREADED & SIMMERED &

CHILI-BAKED CHICKEN WINGS

Preparation time: About 10 minutes

Baking time: About 30 minutes

A golden, crunchy coating with just the right amount of chili seasoning makes these baked drummettes (the meatiest part of the wing) perfect party fare. Serve them hot or cold.

- 2 tablespoons butter or margarine
- 1 tablespoon salad oil
- 1¼ pounds chicken drummettes (about 15 drummettes)
- ¼ cup all-purpose flour
- 2 tablespoons yellow cornmeal
- 1½ teaspoons chili powder
- ½ teaspoon ground cumin

Place butter and oil in a shallow 10- by 15-inch baking pan. Set pan in a 400° oven until butter is melted.

Meanwhile, rinse drummettes and pat dry; set aside. In a paper or plastic bag, combine flour, cornmeal, chili powder, and cumin. Shake drummettes in bag to coat lightly with flour mixture; arrange in a single layer in pan, turning to coat with butter mixture.

Bake, uncovered, until meat near bone is no longer pink; cut to test (about 30 minutes). Serve hot. Or, to serve wings cold, let cool; then cover and refrigerate for at least 4 hours or until next day. Makes about 15 appetizers.

Per appetizer: 83 calories, 6 g protein, 3 g carbohydrates, 5 g fat, 2 g saturated fat, 29 mg cholesterol, 43 mg sodium

GLAZED CHICKEN WINGS ORIENTAL

Preparation time: About 25 minutes

Baking time: About 45 minutes

Two-step baking turns out chicken wings that are crisp and saucy at the same time. Serve them as an appetizer; or, for a full meal, allow three or four wings per person and offer hot rice and Chinese pea pods alongside.

- 2 teaspoons water
- ½ cup cornstarch
- 2 pounds chicken wings
- 1 large egg
- 1 tablespoon salad oil
- ½ cup *each* sugar and regular-strength chicken broth
- ½ cup rice vinegar or white wine vinegar
- ¼ cup catsup
- 1 teaspoon soy sauce
- 2 cloves garlic, minced or pressed

In a small dish, stir together water and 2 teaspoons of the cornstarch. Set aside.

Cut off and discard chicken wingtips; then rinse chicken and pat dry. In a shallow pan, beat egg until blended. Dip wings in egg to coat, then dip in remaining cornstarch to coat lightly. Pour oil into a shallow 10- by 15-inch baking pan; set pan in a 450° oven until oil is hot. Then arrange wings in a single layer in pan. Bake, uncovered, until lightly browned on bottom (about 20 minutes). Turn wings over; continue to bake,

uncovered, until lightly browned on other side (about 20 more minutes). Remove baking pan from oven; drain off fat.

When wings are nearly done, prepare sauce. In a 1½- to 2-quart pan, mix sugar, broth, vinegar, catsup, soy, and garlic. Bring to a boil over high heat; boil, stirring, until reduced to ¾ cup. Stir cornstarch mixture and add to broth mixture; bring to a rolling boil, stirring constantly.

Brush all the sauce over wings. Continue to bake, uncovered, until sauce is bubbly (about 5 more minutes). Makes about 1 dozen appetizers.

Per appetizer: 151 calories, 8 g protein, 13 g carbohydrates, 7 g fat, 2 g saturated fat, 42 mg cholesterol, 158 mg sodium

CHICKEN LIVER CREATIONS

If you like the hearty, robust flavor of chicken livers, you'll want to add these two recipes to your files. Both dishes showcase livers at their best: cooked just until browned outside, but still pink inside.

COUNTRY CHICKEN LIVERS

Preparation time: About 15 minutes

Cooking time: About 10 minutes

   About 1 pound mustard greens
8 slices thick-cut bacon, cut into halves
1 pound chicken livers, drained, cut into halves
1 large onion, sliced
8 ounces mushrooms, sliced
1 tablespoon *each* dry white wine and Worcestershire

Wash and drain mustard greens. Discard tough stems; cut leaves into wide strips and set aside.

Cook bacon in a 10- to 12-inch frying pan over medium heat until crisp (about 10 minutes); lift out and drain. Pour off and discard all but 3 tablespoons of the drippings, then pour 1 tablespoon of the reserved drippings into a 5- to 6-quart pan and set aside.

Add chicken livers to remaining 2 tablespoons drippings in frying pan. Cook over medium-high heat, turning as needed, until browned on outside but still pink in center; cut to test (about 5 minutes). Remove livers from pan and set aside.

Add onion and mushrooms to frying pan; pour in wine and Worcestershire. Cover and cook for 15 minutes, then uncover and continue to cook until almost all liquid has evaporated (about 10 more minutes). Meanwhile, place the 5- to 6-quart pan over medium-high heat; add mustard greens and stir until wilted. Mound greens in center of a platter and keep warm.

Return livers to frying pan with onion and mushrooms; cook, stirring, just until heated through. Spoon liver mixture around greens; garnish with bacon. Makes 4 servings.

Per serving: 393 calories, 32 g protein, 15 g carbohydrates, 23 g fat, 8 g saturated fat, 523 mg cholesterol, 548 mg sodium

LIVERS WITH PEA PODS

Preparation time: About 10 minutes, plus 15 minutes to stand

Cooking time: About 5 minutes

1 pound chicken livers, drained, quartered
1 tablespoon *each* soy sauce and dry sherry
1 tablespoon minced fresh ginger
   Cooking Sauce (recipe follows)
2 tablespoons salad oil
8 ounces Chinese pea pods (also called snow peas), ends and strings removed
6 green onions (including tops), cut into 2-inch lengths
   Hot cooked rice

In a bowl, combine chicken livers, soy, sherry, and 2 teaspoons of the ginger. Stir gently to mix; then let stand for 15 minutes. Meanwhile, prepare Cooking Sauce and set aside.

Heat oil in a wok or 12- to 14-inch frying pan over high heat. Add pea pods, remaining 1 teaspoon ginger, and onions; cook, stirring, until pea pods turn bright green and are tender to bite (about 1 minute). Remove from pan with a slotted spoon and set aside.

Add livers and their marinade to pan. Cook, stirring, until livers are browned on outside but still pink in center; cut to test (about 3 minutes). Return pea pod mixture to pan; then add Cooking Sauce. Cook, stirring, just until ingredients are well blended and sauce is thickened. Serve over rice. Makes 4 servings.

COOKING SAUCE. In a small bowl, stir together 2 tablespoons *each* **soy sauce** and **dry sherry** and 1 teaspoon *each* **sugar** and **cornstarch**.

Per serving: 252 calories, 23 g protein, 14 g carbohydrates, 11 g fat, 2 g saturated fat, 498 mg cholesterol, 866 mg sodium

■ *Pictured on facing page*

SPICY CHICKEN WINGS

Preparation time: About 15 minutes

Baking time: About 45 minutes

Our version of this popular appetizer makes enough to let a crowd keep coming back for more. True fire-eaters will enjoy the super-hot nibbles served plain—but most diners will appreciate the chance to soothe their tastebuds with side-snacks of celery sticks and cool, creamy blue cheese dip.

    4 **pounds chicken wings, cut apart at joints**
       Red Hot Sauce (recipe follows)
       Blue Cheese Dip (optional; recipe follows)
    2 **bunches celery (about 2 lbs. *total*), optional**

Discard chicken wingtips. Rinse remaining wing pieces and pat dry, then arrange in a single layer in 2 lightly greased shallow 10- by 15-inch baking pans. Bake, uncovered, in a 400° oven until golden brown (about 30 minutes).

Meanwhile, prepare Red Hot Sauce. Remove pans from oven, drain off fat, and pour sauce over chicken; turn chicken to coat well. Then continue to bake, uncovered, turning wings once or twice, until sauce is bubbly and edges of wings are crisp (about 15 more minutes).

Meanwhile, if desired, prepare Blue Cheese Dip and break celery stalks from bunches; remove leaves and set aside. Slice stalks lengthwise and place in a bowl.

Arrange chicken on a platter. If using celery and Blue Cheese Dip, garnish chicken with reserved celery leaves; offer with celery stalks and dip. Makes about 4 dozen appetizers.

RED HOT SAUCE. In a small bowl, stir together ½ cup *each* **distilled white vinegar** and **water,** ¼ cup **tomato paste,** 4 teaspoons **sugar,** 1 to 3 tablespoons (or to taste) **liquid hot pepper seasoning,** and 1 to 3 teaspoons (or to taste) **ground red pepper** (cayenne).

Per appetizer without dip: 45 calories, 4 g protein, 1 g carbohydrates, 3 g fat, 1 g saturated fat, 12 mg cholesterol, 39 mg sodium

BLUE CHEESE DIP. In a bowl, coarsely mash 4 ounces **blue-veined cheese.** Stir in 1 cup **sour cream,** 1 teaspoon minced **garlic,** ½ teaspoon **dry mustard,** and ⅛ teaspoon **pepper.** If made ahead, cover and refrigerate for up to 3 days. Makes 1⅓ cups.

Per tablespoon: 43 calories, 2 g protein, 1 g carbohydrates, 4 g fat, 2 g saturated fat, 9 mg cholesterol, 81 mg sodium

BASIL PARMESAN CHICKEN WINGS

Preparation time: About 20 minutes

Baking time: About 30 minutes

Here's a great way to start an Italian feast. Coat chicken drummettes with garlic butter, then roll in cheese- and basil-seasoned crumbs and bake until crisp.

    ¼ **cup butter or margarine**
    2 **tablespoons salad oil**
    1 **clove garlic, minced or pressed**
    1 **cup soft bread crumbs**
    2 **tablespoons finely chopped parsley**
    ½ **cup grated Parmesan cheese**
    ¼ **cup grated Romano cheese**
    1 **teaspoon dry basil leaves**
  1½ **pounds chicken drummettes (about 18 drummettes)**

In a frying pan or other shallow pan, combine butter, oil, and garlic. Stir over low heat until butter is melted. In another shallow pan or wide, shallow rimmed plate, combine crumbs, parsley, Parmesan cheese, Romano cheese, and basil.

Rinse drummettes and pat dry. Dip each drummette in butter mixture to coat; then roll in crumb mixture to coat.

Arrange chicken in a single layer in a lightly greased shallow 10- by 15-inch baking pan. Bake, uncovered, in a 400° oven until meat near bone is no longer pink; cut to test (about 30 minutes). Makes about 1½ dozen appetizers.

Per appetizer: 99 calories, 6 g protein, 1 g carbohydrates, 7 g fat, 3 g saturated fat, 31 mg cholesterol, 114 mg sodium

Serve Spicy Chicken Wings (recipe on facing page) at
your next appetizer party—and start the evening off with a bang!
A tomato-based hot sauce, fiery with cayenne and liquid hot pepper
seasoning, coats the wings as they bake.

HOT CHILI CHICKEN WINGS

Preparation time: About 10 minutes

Cooking time: About 45 minutes

Combine soy sauce with chili oil, add garlic and fresh ginger, and simmer drummettes in the mixture until it's reduced to a thick (and incendiary!) glaze. Serve hot, or refrigerate and serve cold the next day.

- 2 **pounds chicken drummettes (about 24 drummettes)**
- 2 **tablespoons salad oil**
- ¼ **cup soy sauce**
- 2 **tablespoons rice wine or dry sherry**
- 2 **tablespoons sugar**
- 1 **teaspoon chili oil or 2 small dried hot red chiles**
- 4 **quarter-size slices fresh ginger**
- 2 **cloves garlic**
- 2 **green onions, roots and tops trimmed**
- 1 **cup water**

Rinse drummettes and pat dry. Heat salad oil in a 10- to 12-inch frying pan over medium-high heat. Add drummettes, a portion at a time; cook, turning as needed, until browned on all sides (about 6 minutes).

Return all chicken to pan; add soy, wine, sugar, chili oil, ginger, garlic, onions, and water. Bring to a boil. Then reduce heat, cover, and simmer until meat near bone is no longer pink; cut to test (about 20 minutes). Uncover and bring to a boil; boil, turning chicken often, until sauce is reduced and thick enough to coat chicken (about 10 minutes). If made ahead, let cool; then cover and refrigerate until next day. Serve hot or cold. Makes about 2 dozen appetizers.

Per appetizer: 60 calories, 5 g protein, 2 g carbohydrates, 4 g fat, 1 g saturated fat, 21 mg cholesterol, 193 mg sodium

GRILLED MUSTARD WINGS & RIBS

Preparation time: About 10 minutes

Marinating time: At least 4 hours or up to 1 day

Grilling time: About 20 minutes

Forget the utensils at your next patio party: these are strictly finger foods. Chicken wings and meaty beef ribs, bathed in a mustardy marinade, cook together on the grill.

- **Mustard Marinade (recipe follows)**
- 3 **pounds chicken wings**
- 3 **pounds beef ribs, cut into separate ribs**

Prepare Mustard Marinade; set aside. Cut off and discard chicken wingtips; then rinse chicken and pat dry.

Place chicken and ribs in separate large heavy-duty plastic bags. Pour half the marinade into each bag. Seal bags and turn over several times to coat meat with marinade; then set bags in a large, shallow baking pan or dish. Refrigerate for at least 4 hours or up to 1 day, turning bags over several times.

Drain chicken and ribs; reserve marinade. Place meats on a lightly greased grill 4 to 6 inches above a solid bed of medium-hot coals. Cook chicken, turning occasionally and basting with marinade, until browned on outside and no longer pink near bone; cut to test (about 20 minutes). Cook ribs, turning and basting, until browned on outside but still slightly pink near bone; cut to test (about 15 minutes). Makes 6 servings.

MUSTARD MARINADE. In a bowl, stir together 1 cup **Dijon mustard,** 1 cup **dry white wine** or regular-strength chicken broth, 2 tablespoons *each* **salad oil** and **honey,** 2 teaspoons **dry tarragon leaves,** and 2 cloves **garlic,** minced or pressed.

Per serving: 608 calories, 43 g protein, 6 g carbohydrates, 45 g fat, 15 g saturated fat, 145 mg cholesterol, 727 mg sodium

■ *Pictured on page 82*

OVEN-FRIED TURKEY WINGS

Preparation time: About 15 minutes

Baking time: About 40 minutes

Cornmeal-crunchy turkey wings are fun to pick up and eat with your fingers—and they're easy to "fry" in the oven.

    6 turkey wings (about 5 lbs. *total*)
1¼ cups yellow cornmeal
    2 tablespoons paprika
    1 tablespoon dry marjoram leaves
    1 teaspoon pepper
    1 large egg
    2 tablespoons water
      About 5 tablespoons butter or margarine, melted
      Salt

With your hands, force joints of each turkey wing open until they snap; then cut wings apart at joints.

Discard wingtips. Rinse remaining wing pieces and pat dry.

In a wide, shallow rimmed plate, mix cornmeal, paprika, marjoram, and pepper. In a shallow pan, beat egg and water to blend.

Dip wing pieces in egg mixture to coat; then dip in cornmeal mixture to coat well (pat coating on lightly for an extra-thick crust). Arrange pieces, slightly apart, in a single layer in an oiled shallow 10- by 15-inch baking pan.

Bake, uncovered, in a 400° oven for 15 minutes; drizzle evenly with butter. Continue to bake, uncovered, until meat near bone in thickest part of wing is no longer pink; cut to test (about 25 more minutes). Season to taste with salt. Makes 6 servings.

Per serving: 688 calories, 68 g protein, 24 g carbohydrates, 34 g fat, 13 g saturated fat, 327 mg cholesterol, 279 mg sodium

HOISIN TURKEY WINGS

Preparation time: About 10 minutes

Marinating time: At least 1 hour or up to 1 day

Grilling time: About 45 minutes

A few simple ingredients and half a dozen turkey wings add up to an easy entrée that leaves you with plenty of time to relax. Accompany the barbecued turkey with grilled green onions and fresh fruit salad.

    1 cup hoisin sauce
  ⅓ cup dry sherry
  ¼ cup lemon juice
    3 cloves garlic, minced or pressed
    6 turkey wings (about 5 lbs. *total*)

In a shallow pan or dish, combine hoisin, sherry, lemon juice, and garlic. Cut off and discard turkey wingtips; then rinse turkey, pat dry, and add to marinade. Turn to coat. Cover and refrigerate for at least 1 hour or up to 1 day.

Drain turkey; reserve marinade. Place turkey on a lightly greased grill 4 to 6 inches above a solid bed of medium-hot coals. Cook, turning occasionally and basting with marinade, until meat near bone in thickest part of wing is no longer pink; cut to test (about 45 minutes). Makes 6 servings.

Per serving: 513 calories, 65 g protein, 8 g carbohydrates, 23 g fat, 6 g saturated fat, 265 mg cholesterol, 850 mg sodium

*When our Sour Cream Meatballs (recipe on page 92) are on
the menu, expect guests to linger over lunch. Serve the delicate meatballs
over your favorite pasta shapes; we chose bowties. Spinach-stuffed
tomatoes make a colorful side dish.*

Versatile Ground Meat

CRUMBLED & SEASONED & PEPPERED & BAKED &

NUTTED & POCKETED & PATTIED & LAYERED &

LOAFED & SCENTED & SANDWICHED & STACKED &

■ *Pictured on page 90*

SOUR CREAM MEATBALLS

Preparation time: About 15 minutes

Cooking time: About 40 minutes

Novices and accomplished cooks alike will present this dish with pride. Delicate ground chicken meatballs flavored with rye bread crumbs and a hint of mustard are first browned, then simmered in a rich tomato–sour cream sauce.

1½	**pounds ground chicken**
1	**cup rye bread crumbs**
1	**small onion, finely chopped**
⅓	**cup finely chopped parsley**
1	**large egg**
1	**teaspoon dry mustard**
¼	**teaspoon pepper**
2	**tablespoons salad oil**
1½	**cups regular-strength chicken broth**
1	**can (6 oz.) tomato paste**
2	**cups sour cream**
	Hot cooked pasta

In a large bowl, combine chicken, crumbs, onion, ¼ cup of the parsley, egg, mustard, and pepper. Mix thoroughly; then shape into 1-inch balls.

Heat oil in a 12- to 14-inch frying pan over medium-high heat. Add meatballs, a portion at a time; do not crowd pan. Cook, turning often, until no longer pink in center; cut to test (about 10 minutes).

In a 4-quart pan, blend broth and tomato paste; bring to a boil over medium-high heat. Gradually stir in sour cream. Reduce heat to medium-low, add meatballs, and simmer, uncovered, stirring occasionally, for 15 minutes. Serve over pasta and sprinkle with remaining parsley. Makes 6 servings.

Per serving: 447 calories, 26 g protein, 14 g carbohydrates, 32 g fat, 13 g saturated fat, 163 mg cholesterol, 662 mg sodium

SUNSHINE STUFFED PEPPERS

Preparation time: About 55 minutes

Baking time: About 30 minutes

Quick cure for rainy day blues: Sunny bell peppers stuffed with tomatoes, chicken, and provolone cheese. The bright red "surprise packages," their filling seasoned with garlic, oregano, fennel seeds, and chiles, will wake up your palate and lift your spirits.

8	**medium-size red bell peppers**
2	**tablespoons salad oil**
2	**large onions, sliced**
3	**cloves garlic, minced or pressed**
1½	**pounds ground chicken**
¾	**cup chopped Italian parsley**
1	**teaspoon *each* dry oregano leaves and fennel seeds**
¼	**teaspoon crushed dried hot red chiles**
2	**small tomatoes, peeled and chopped**
8	**ounces provolone cheese, cut into ½-inch cubes**
1	**cup cooked brown rice**

Cut off and discard stem ends of bell peppers, then remove seeds. If necessary, trim bases of peppers so they will stand upright. In a 6- to 8-quart pan, bring 3 to 4 quarts water to a boil over high heat. Add peppers and cook for 2 minutes, then lift out and plunge into cold water to cool. Drain and set aside.

Heat oil in a 12- to 14-inch frying pan over medium heat. Add onions and garlic and cook, stirring occasionally, until onions are soft (about 10 minutes). Add chicken and cook, stirring often, until no longer pink (about 10 minutes). Remove from heat and let cool; then mix in parsley, oregano, fennel seeds, chiles, tomatoes, cheese, and rice.

Fill peppers equally with chicken mixture and arrange upright in a shallow 1½-quart baking dish. Bake, uncovered, in a 350° oven until cheese is melted and stuffing is lightly browned on top (about 30 minutes). Makes 8 servings.

Per serving: 324 calories, 24 g protein, 14 g carbohydrates, 19 g fat, 7 g saturated fat, 90 mg cholesterol, 325 mg sodium

TARRAGON CHICKEN TURNOVERS

Preparation time: About 1 hour

Baking time: About 15 minutes

Give your family or friends some extra attention of the edible kind—put together an individual main-dish pie for each person. Brush your favorite pastry with tarragon mustard; then fill with ham, cheese, chicken, and mushrooms, and bake.

- 2 tablespoons butter or margarine
- 2 tablespoons *each* minced onion and minced shallots
- 8 ounces mushrooms, chopped
- 1 pound ground chicken
- 2 ounces cooked ham, finely chopped
- 2 tablespoons finely chopped parsley
- ¼ teaspoon pepper
- ¼ cup whipping cream
- 1 cup (4 oz.) shredded Swiss cheese
  Pastry for 2 double-crust 9-inch pies
- ¼ cup tarragon mustard
- 1 large egg yolk beaten with 2 tablespoons milk

Melt butter in a 12- to 14-inch frying pan over medium-high heat. Add onion, shallots, and mushrooms; cook, stirring often, until onion and shallots are golden brown (about 15 minutes). Add chicken and ham; cook, stirring often, until chicken is no longer pink (about 5 minutes). Add parsley, pepper, and cream; continue to cook until mixture is thickened (about 5 minutes). Remove from heat, let cool, and stir in cheese.

On a lightly floured board, roll out pastry to a thickness of ⅛ inch. Cut out eight 6-inch circles. Brush each circle evenly with 1½ teaspoons of the mustard, then mound an eighth of the chicken mixture in center of each circle. Fold pastry over filling, press edges to seal, and brush with egg yolk mixture. Place turnovers, slightly apart, on a baking sheet. Bake, uncovered, in a 425° oven until lightly browned (about 15 minutes). Makes 8 servings.

Per serving: 494 calories, 21 g protein, 27 g carbohydrates, 33 g fat, 12 g saturated fat, 107 mg cholesterol, 438 mg sodium

CHICKEN EGGPLANT PARMESAN

Preparation time: About 45 minutes

Baking time: About 25 minutes

It's time to add another version of hearty, ever-popular eggplant *parmigiana* to your recipe files. The meaty tomato sauce is made with ground chicken; the eggplant slices are oven-browned, not fried, letting you use a minimum of oil.

- Oven-browned Eggplant (recipe follows)
- 1 tablespoon olive oil
- 1½ pounds ground chicken
- 2 cloves garlic, minced or pressed
- 1 large can (15 oz.) tomato sauce
- 2 teaspoons dry oregano leaves
- 1 teaspoon dry thyme leaves
- ½ teaspoon dry marjoram leaves
- 1 cup (about 5 oz.) grated Parmesan cheese
- ¼ cup chopped Italian parsley

Prepare Oven-browned Eggplant; set aside.

While eggplant is baking, heat oil in a 12- to 14-inch frying pan over medium-high heat. Add chicken

and garlic; cook, stirring often, until chicken is no longer pink (about 5 minutes). Stir in tomato sauce, oregano, thyme, and marjoram; reduce heat to medium-low and simmer for about 5 minutes. Remove from heat.

Arrange half the Oven-browned Eggplant in a shallow 2- to 2½-quart baking dish. Cover with half the chicken-tomato sauce; sprinkle with ½ cup of the cheese. Repeat layers, using remaining eggplant, sauce, and cheese. Sprinkle with parsley. Cover and bake in a 375° oven for 20 minutes; then uncover and continue to bake until lightly browned (about 5 more minutes). Makes 6 servings.

OVEN-BROWNED EGGPLANT. Cut 1 large **eggplant** (about 1¾ lbs.) into ¼-inch-thick slices. Brush slices with **olive oil** (you'll need about ⅓ cup). Arrange slices in a single layer in 2 shallow baking pans. Bake, uncovered, in a 425° oven until browned (about 25 minutes), turning slices over halfway through baking to brown evenly. Season to taste with **salt** and **pepper.**

Per serving: 467 calories, 32 g protein, 15 g carbohydrates, 31 g fat, 9 g saturated fat, 113 mg cholesterol, 966 mg sodium

SWEET SPICE CHICKEN & ORZO

Preparation time: About 10 minutes

Cooking time: About 1¾ hours

Not your typical tomato sauce, this chunky, slow-simmered blend of bacon, onions, celery, and chicken is richly seasoned with herbs and sweet spices. Serve it with tiny rice-shaped pasta.

  4 **ounces sliced bacon, chopped**
  1 **pound ground chicken**
  4 **medium-size onions, chopped**
  2 **cloves garlic, minced or pressed**
  1 **cup finely chopped celery**
     Spice Blend (recipe follows)
  2 **tablespoons finely chopped parsley**
  3 **large cans (15 oz. *each*) tomato sauce**
  1 **can (6 oz.) tomato paste**
  2 **tablespoons red wine vinegar**
  1 **pound dry orzo or other tiny pasta shapes**

Cook bacon in a 5- to 6-quart pan over medium-high heat until lightly browned (about 10 minutes), stirring occasionally. Spoon off and discard all but 2 tablespoons of the drippings. Then add chicken and cook, stirring often, until no longer pink (about 5 minutes). Add onions, garlic, and celery; cook, stirring often, until onions are very soft (about 20 minutes). Meanwhile, prepare Spice Blend.

To chicken mixture, add Spice Blend, parsley, tomato sauce, tomato paste, and vinegar. Bring to a boil; then reduce heat to medium-low and simmer, uncovered, until sauce is thickened and flavors are blended (about 1 hour).

Cook orzo according to package directions just until tender to bite. Drain well; place in a large, shallow serving bowl and top with chicken-tomato sauce. Mix lightly. Makes 8 to 10 servings.

SPICE BLEND. In a small bowl, mix 1 tablespoon firmly packed **brown sugar;** ½ teaspoon *each* **ground cinnamon, dry oregano leaves, pepper, dry sage leaves,** and **dry thyme leaves;** and ¼ teaspoon *each* **ground cloves** and **ground nutmeg.**

Per serving: 387 calories, 20 g protein, 57 g carbohydrates, 10 g fat, 3 g saturated fat, 47 mg cholesterol, 1,136 mg sodium

CHICKEN IN CREAMY PEANUT SAUCE

Preparation time: About 10 minutes

Cooking time: About 15 minutes

It may be ready in minutes, but it's not missing a thing! This stir-fry has it all—fantastic flavor, and speed and ease of preparation. The spicy peanut sauce, packed with meat and vegetables, is served with soba noodles (or use whole wheat spaghetti, if you like).

       Creamy Peanut Sauce (recipe follows)
   1   **tablespoon salad oil**
   1   **large onion, sliced**
   1   **clove garlic, minced or pressed**
  1½   **pounds ground chicken**
  12   **ounces dry soba noodles**
   2   **cups shredded napa cabbage**
   ¼   **cup chopped green onions (including tops)**

Prepare Creamy Peanut Sauce and set aside.

Heat oil in a 12- to 14-inch frying pan over medium-high heat. Add sliced onion and garlic; cook, stirring often, until onion is soft (about 7 minutes). Add chicken and cook, stirring often, until no longer pink (about 5 minutes).

Meanwhile, cook soba according to package directions just until barely tender to bite. Drain well, place in a large, shallow serving bowl, and keep warm.

Add Creamy Peanut Sauce and cabbage to chicken mixture; bring to a boil, stirring. Stir chicken mixture into drained soba; sprinkle with green onions. Makes 6 servings.

CREAMY PEANUT SAUCE. In a bowl, stir together ½ cup *each* **low-sodium chicken broth** and **reduced-sodium soy sauce;** ¼ cup *each* **creamy peanut butter** and **hoisin sauce;** 1 tablespoon **sugar;** and ½ teaspoon **crushed dried hot red chiles.**

Per serving: 500 calories, 33 g protein, 54 g carbohydrates, 18 g fat, 4 g saturated fat, 94 mg cholesterol, 1,734 mg sodium

*A cluster of your favorite fresh herbs garnishes Sweet Spice
Chicken & Orzo (recipe on facing page). Served over rice-shaped pasta,
the tempting tomato sauce is thick with chicken, celery, onion, and bacon.
A mixed green salad with cucumber slices and tangy feta cheese offers
a refreshing contrast to the richly flavored main course.*

EXTRAORDINARY DUCK ENTRÉES

Duck demands attention and praise at your dinner table. Rich-tasting Peking or Long Island duck, the most popular and widely available variety, is often sold both fresh and frozen in supermarkets. Wild or farm-raised mallard duck is leaner and stronger in flavor than the Peking type; you can order it from specialty markets or—in season—request it from a hunter friend.

When preparing Peking duck for roasting, prick the skin all over with a fork to let the fat drain out; then prick again every 15 minutes throughout the cooking time to allow continued release of fat. For extra-crisp skin, separate the skin from the breast meat by sliding a spoon between the two before roasting.

The recipes we offer here cover several cooking styles and presentations. Our golden roast Duck in Fruit Sauce, basted with honey butter and served with mixed dried fruit and sweet-sour red cabbage, is a beautiful entrée that's sure to take the chill off winter weather. In spring or summer, you may want to try our salad of shredded duck and mixed greens in a tarragon mustard vinaigrette; it can be made with home-cooked or purchased Chinese barbecued duck. To usher in autumn, serve wild duck—first marinated in chile-accented soy sauce, then quickly grilled.

DUCK IN FRUIT SAUCE

Preparation time: About 15 minutes

Cooking time: About 2¾ hours

    1   duck (4½ to 5 lbs.), thawed if frozen
    ¼   cup butter or margarine
    ½   cup honey
    ¼   cup firmly packed brown sugar
    1   package (8 oz.) mixed dried fruit
    1⅓ cups water
        Sweet-Sour Red Cabbage (recipe follows)

Reserve duck neck and giblets for other uses. Pull off and discard lumps of fat from duck; then rinse duck inside and out and pat dry. Secure neck skin to back with a small metal skewer; bend wings akimbo.

With a fork, prick duck skin all over. Then place duck, breast down, on a rack in a 12- by 15-inch roasting pan. Roast, uncovered, in a 350° oven for 1 hour. Turn duck breast up and continue to roast, uncovered, for 45 more minutes.

Meanwhile, melt butter in a 1- to 1½-quart pan over medium heat. Stir in honey and sugar; cook, stirring, until sugar is dissolved. Remove from heat and set aside.

Place dried fruit in another 1- to 1½-quart pan, add water, and bring to a boil. Cover, remove from heat, and let stand until duck is ready. Also prepare Sweet-Sour Red Cabbage and set aside.

After duck has roasted for 1¾ hours, siphon off and discard all fat from roasting pan. Reduce oven temperature to 300°. Continue to roast duck until meat near thighbone is no longer pink; cut to test (about 45 more minutes). During first 20 minutes, baste duck 3 or 4 times with butter-honey mixture.

Transfer duck to a platter; discard fat in roasting pan. Pour remaining butter-honey mixture into pan; bring to a boil over medium-high heat, stirring to scrape up browned bits. Reduce heat to low. Drain fruit and turn gently in roasting pan to warm and mix with sauce. Also reheat Sweet-Sour Red Cabbage.

Spoon fruit sauce around duck on platter; serve duck and fruit with cabbage. Makes 4 servings.

Per serving without cabbage: 1,110 calories, 41 g protein, 84 g carbohydrates, 70 g fat, 27 g saturated fat, 203 mg cholesterol, 254 mg sodium

SWEET-SOUR RED CABBAGE. Core and finely shred 1 medium-size head **red cabbage** (about 2 lbs.). Place cabbage in a 5- to 6-quart pan and add ½ cup **water**, ⅓ cup **cider vinegar**, 1 tablespoon *each* **granulated sugar** and firmly packed **brown sugar,** and ¼ teaspoon **pepper.** Bring to a boil over high heat; then reduce heat, cover, and simmer, stirring occasionally, until cabbage is very tender to bite (about 40 minutes). Uncover and boil rapidly, stirring, until any liquid has evaporated. Makes 4 cups.

Per cup: 77 calories, 3 g protein, 19 g carbohydrates, 0 g fat, 0 g saturated fat, 0 mg cholesterol, 21 mg sodium

DUCK & GREENS IN VINAIGRETTE

Preparation time: About 35 minutes

Baking time: About 2½ hours

Cooked Duck (recipe follows); or 1 Chinese barbecued duck (2 to 2½ lbs.)

House Dressing (recipe follows)

8 to 12 ounces green or red leaf lettuce, separated into leaves, washed, and crisped

About 8 ounces *each* escarole and chicory (or 1 pound escarole or chicory), separated into leaves, washed, and crisped

About 8 ounces radicchio, separated into leaves, washed, and crisped

Salt and pepper

Prepare Cooked Duck. Pull meat from duck; discard skin and bones. Tear meat into thin shreds.

Prepare House Dressing and set aside.

Line a salad bowl with large lettuce leaves. Tear remaining lettuce into bite-size pieces; coarsely chop escarole and chicory. Add torn lettuce, escarole, chicory, and radicchio to bowl. Top greens with duck, add House Dressing, and mix well. Season to taste with salt and pepper. Makes 6 to 8 servings.

COOKED DUCK. Use 1 **duck** (4½ to 5 lbs.), thawed if frozen. Reserve duck neck and giblets for other uses; pull off and discard lumps of fat from duck. Rinse duck inside and out; pat dry.

Wrap duck in foil and place in a 9- by 13-inch baking pan. Bake in a 350° oven until meat is tender enough to pull easily from bones (about 2½ hours). Unwrap and let cool.

HOUSE DRESSING. In a small bowl, stir together 1 teaspoon **dry tarragon leaves,** 1 tablespoon **mustard**

seeds, ¼ cup **Dijon mustard,** ½ cup **balsamic vinegar** or red wine vinegar, ½ cup **olive oil** or salad oil, and 1 small **red onion,** thinly slivered.

Per serving: 580 calories, 25 g protein, 8 g carbohydrates, 50 g fat, 13 g saturated fat, 98 mg cholesterol, 355 mg sodium

GRILLED MALLARD DUCKS WITH SOY

Preparation time: About 45 minutes

Marinating time: At least 30 minutes or up to 2 hours

Grilling time: About 10 minutes

4 wild or farm-raised mallard ducks (1½ to 2 lbs. *each*)

3 cloves garlic, minced or pressed

¾ cup light soy sauce

¼ teaspoon crushed dried hot red chiles

2 lemons, cut into wedges

½ cup canned lingonberries, drained

About 2 cups watercress sprigs, washed and crisped

With poultry shears or a heavy knife, cut ducks in half lengthwise. Remove backbones. Cut off wings.

On each duck half, start at edge of breast and slide a small, sharp knife parallel to bone, cutting meat free from bones of breast and back. Then cut thigh from body, so you end up with boned body meat with a leg attached. Trim off any loose skin flaps. If breast fillets fall free, reserve them.

Reserve wings and bones for stock, if desired. Rinse duck halves and pat dry. Press breast fillets back in place, if necessary.

Place duck halves in a large heavy-duty plastic bag. Add garlic, soy, and chiles. Seal bag and turn over several times to coat duck halves with marinade. Place bag in a large, shallow baking pan or dish; refrigerate for at least 30 minutes or up to 2 hours, turning bag over several times.

Drain duck; discard marinade. Then lay duck halves out flat, skin side down, on a lightly greased grill 4 to 6 inches above a solid bed of hot coals. Cook, turning as needed to brown evenly, until breast meat in thickest part is pinkish-red but no longer wet-looking; cut to test (about 10 minutes). Place duck on a platter.

To serve, garnish duck with lemon wedges, lingonberries, and watercress. Makes 4 servings.

Per serving: 1,099 calories, 60 g protein, 22 g carbohydrates, 86 g fat, 29 g saturated fat, 254 mg cholesterol*

*Sodium data not available.

Easy to prepare and simple to serve, Layered Turkey Enchiladas (recipe on facing page) are good for you, too! To assemble the tempting tower, just stack corn tortillas with a blend of ground turkey, chiles, cheese, tomatoes, and salsa. Serve with simmered pinto beans and more salsa, if you like.

SUMMER CHICKEN STIR-FRY

Preparation time: About 10 minutes, plus 1 hour to soak bulgur

Cooking time: About 12 minutes

Summer meals can present a dilemma. When the weather's sultry, you don't want to spend much time in the kitchen—but you still may be in the mood for a hot dinner. Solve the problem with this simple combination of ground chicken, zucchini, and carrots, easily stir-fried in under 15 minutes. There's no need to steam rice to go alongside; you serve the dish over bulgur that's soaked, not cooked, to tenderness.

1 **cup bulgur (cracked wheat)**
2 **cups boiling water**
  Cooking Sauce (recipe follows)
2 **tablespoons olive oil or salad oil**
3 **cloves garlic, minced or pressed**
1 **pound ground chicken**
2 **cups thinly sliced carrots**
2 **small zucchini, thinly sliced**
1 **tablespoon minced fresh ginger**
⅓ **cup water**
½ **cup thinly sliced green onions (including tops)**

In a bowl, stir together bulgur and the 2 cups boiling water; set aside until almost all liquid has been absorbed (about 1 hour). Drain.

Prepare Cooking Sauce and set aside.

Heat oil in a wok or 12- to 14-inch frying pan over high heat. Add garlic and chicken; cook, stirring often, until chicken is lightly browned (about 5 minutes). Remove chicken mixture from pan and set aside.

To pan, add carrots, zucchini, ginger, and the ⅓ cup water; stir to scrape up browned bits. Cover; cook until vegetables are tender to bite (about 5 minutes), stirring often. Then uncover and boil until almost all liquid has evaporated. Add chicken mixture and Cooking Sauce; bring to a boil, stirring.

Spoon bulgur onto plates; top with chicken mixture and sprinkle with onions. Makes 4 servings.

COOKING SAUCE. In a small bowl, stir together ½ cup **regular-strength chicken broth,** 2 tablespoons **soy sauce,** and 1 tablespoon **cornstarch.**

Per serving: 109 calories, 27 g protein, 38 g carbohydrates, 18 g fat, 4 g saturated fat, 94 mg cholesterol, 758 mg sodium

---

■ *Pictured on facing page*

LAYERED TURKEY ENCHILADAS

Preparation time: About 15 minutes

Baking time: About 1 hour and 20 minutes

These quick, low-fat enchiladas are something like a savory layer cake: you stack up corn tortillas and an appetizing filling of ground turkey breast, green chiles, Cheddar cheese, and mild salsa. To serve the "cake," simply cut it into wedges.

1 **pound ground skinned turkey breast**
1 **large can (7 oz.) diced green chiles**
1 **medium-size onion, chopped**
1 **cup (4 oz.) shredded extra-sharp Cheddar cheese**
1 **cup prepared mild green chile salsa**
1½ **cups chopped pear-shaped tomatoes**
8 **corn tortillas (*each* 6 to 7 inches in diameter)**

In a bowl, mix turkey, chiles, onion, ¾ cup of the cheese, ½ cup of the salsa, and 1 cup of the tomatoes. Divide into 7 equal portions.

Place a tortilla in a shallow 9- to 10-inch-diameter baking pan; cover evenly with one portion of the turkey mixture. Repeat layers to use remaining tortillas and turkey mixture, finishing with a tortilla. Then cover with remaining ¼ cup cheese, ½ cup salsa, and ½ cup tomatoes.

Cover with foil and bake in a 400° oven for 40 minutes. Uncover and continue to bake until turkey is no longer pink; cut to center of stack to test (about 40 more minutes). Let stand for 5 minutes, then cut into wedges. Makes 4 to 6 servings.

Per serving: 341 calories, 31 g protein, 30 g carbohydrates, 11 g fat, 5 g saturated fat, 80 mg cholesterol, 821 mg sodium

TURKEY-PISTACHIO APPETIZER CUPS

Preparation time: About 1 hour

Baking time: About 12 minutes

Looking for an appetizer with a difference? Fresh mint makes a fragrant and flavorful impact on mushrooms stuffed with ground turkey. These tasty mouthfuls are just right for parties, since you can get them all ready to bake a full day in advance.

- 40 **mushrooms (about 2 lbs.** *total***),** *each* **1½ to 2 inches in diameter**
- 3 **tablespoons soy sauce**
- 1 **tablespoon olive oil or salad oil**
- 1 **small onion, finely chopped**
- ½ **cup finely chopped salted roasted pistachio nuts**
- 8 **ounces ground turkey**
- 1 **tablespoon cornstarch**
- 1 **large egg white**
- 3 **tablespoons fine dry bread crumbs**
- ¼ **cup chopped fresh mint**

Carefully break off mushroom stems; mince stems and set aside.

Arrange a third of the mushrooms, stemmed side up, in a 10- to 12-inch frying pan. Sprinkle with 1 tablespoon of the soy. Cook over medium heat until mushroom cups contain liquid (about 3 minutes), then turn mushrooms over and continue to cook until pan is almost dry (about 3 more minutes). Transfer cooked mushrooms, stemmed side up, to an oiled 9- by 13-inch baking dish. Repeat to cook remaining mushrooms in 2 batches, using remaining 2 tablespoons soy.

To frying pan, add oil, onion, and minced mushroom stems. Cook over medium-high heat, stirring often, until onion is soft and all liquid has evaporated (about 7 minutes). Add pistachios and cook, stirring, until mixture is lightly browned; then remove from heat and let cool.

To onion mixture, add turkey, cornstarch, egg white, crumbs, and mint; mix well. Divide mixture into 40 equal portions and shape each into a ball. Set a ball in each mushroom cap and press down to settle firmly in place. (At this point, you may cover and refrigerate for up to 1 day.)

Bake mushrooms, uncovered, in a 500° oven until turkey-pistachio stuffing is no longer pink in center; cut to test (about 12 minutes; about 17 minutes if refrigerated). Serve hot. Makes 40 appetizers.

Per appetizer: 31 calories, 2 g protein, 2 g carbohydrates, 2 g fat, 0 g saturated fat, 4 mg cholesterol, 101 mg sodium

APPLE TURKEY LOAF

Preparation time: About 25 minutes

Baking time: About 1 hour

This moist, apple-filled meat loaf tastes marvelous between thick slices of crunchy-crusted bread. For an especially lean loaf, we've used ground skinned turkey breast in place of regular ground turkey.

- 1 **tablespoon butter or margarine**
- 2 **tart green-skinned apples, such as Granny Smith, peeled, cored, and chopped**
- 1 **medium-size onion, chopped**
- 1½ **pounds ground skinned turkey breast**
- 1½ **teaspoons dry marjoram leaves**
- 1 **teaspoon** *each* **dry thyme leaves, dry sage leaves, and pepper**
- ½ **cup chopped parsley**
- 2 **large egg whites**
- ½ **cup** *each* **fine dry bread crumbs and nonfat milk**

Melt butter in a 10- to 12-inch frying pan over medium heat. Add apples and onion; cook, stirring occasionally, until onion is soft (about 10 minutes). Remove from heat and let cool; then scrape into a large bowl and mix in turkey, marjoram, thyme, sage, pepper, parsley, egg whites, crumbs, and milk. Pat mixture evenly into a 5- by 9-inch loaf pan.

Bake loaf, uncovered, in a 350° oven until browned on top and no longer pink in center; cut to test (about 1 hour). Drain fat from loaf pan, then invert pan and turn loaf out onto a platter. Serve hot. Or, to serve cold, let cool; then cover and refrigerate for up to 1 day. Makes 6 servings.

Per serving: 224 calories, 30 g protein, 15 g carbohydrates, 4 g fat, 2 g saturated fat, 76 mg cholesterol, 188 mg sodium

SHEPHERD'S PIE

Preparation time: About 45 minutes

Baking time: About 20 minutes

Beneath its creamy mashed potato topping, this one-dish dinner holds a surprise: a filling made with ground turkey, not the traditional minced lamb.

- 2 pounds russet potatoes, scrubbed
- 2 tablespoons salad oil
- 1 large onion, chopped
- 2 cloves garlic, minced or pressed
- ½ cup finely chopped celery
- 8 ounces mushrooms, sliced
- 1½ pounds ground turkey
- 2 teaspoons dry sage leaves
- 1 teaspoon dry thyme leaves
- ½ teaspoon *each* dry marjoram leaves and dry mustard
- 8 ounces carrots, shredded
- ⅓ cup chopped parsley
- 1 cup regular-strength chicken broth
- ¼ cup milk
- ½ cup (¼ lb.) butter or margarine, at room temperature
- ¼ teaspoon white pepper
- 1 teaspoon salt

Place whole unpeeled potatoes in a 3-quart pan and add enough water to cover. Bring to a boil over high heat; then reduce heat, cover, and boil gently until potatoes are tender throughout when pierced (about 30 minutes).

Meanwhile, heat oil in a 12- to 14-inch frying pan over medium-high heat. Add onion, garlic, celery, and mushrooms; cook, stirring often, until onion is soft (about 7 minutes). Add turkey and cook, stirring often, until no longer pink (about 5 minutes). Add sage, thyme, marjoram, and mustard; cook for 1 minute. Add carrots, parsley, and broth. Bring to a boil over high heat, then boil until liquid has evaporated (about 10 minutes). Transfer to a 3-quart casserole.

Drain potatoes; peel and mash with milk, butter, pepper, and salt. Spread over turkey mixture. Bake, uncovered, in a 375° oven until lightly browned (about 20 minutes). Makes 6 servings.

Per serving: 512 calories, 25 g protein, 37 g carbohydrates, 30 g fat, 13 g saturated fat, 126 mg cholesterol, 837 mg sodium

TURKEY LASAGNE

Preparation time: About 1 hour

Baking time: About 25 minutes

Ground turkey in the herbed tomato sauce makes for a lasagne that's a bit leaner than the usual dish.

- 1 package (8 oz.) dry lasagne noodles
- 12 ounces carrots, cut into ¼-inch-thick slices
- 1 pound zucchini, cut into ¼-inch-thick slices
- 2 tablespoons olive oil or salad oil
- 1 medium-size onion, chopped
- 1 teaspoon *each* dry basil leaves, dry thyme leaves, and dry oregano leaves
- 8 ounces ground turkey
- 1 jar (32 oz.) marinara sauce
- 2 packages (10 oz. *each*) frozen chopped spinach, thawed and squeezed dry
- 1 cup (8 oz.) ricotta cheese
- 3 cups (12 oz.) shredded mozzarella cheese
- ¼ cup grated Parmesan cheese

In a 5- to 6-quart pan, bring 3 quarts water to a boil over high heat. Add noodles and carrots; cook for 6 minutes. Add zucchini; continue to cook until noodles are just tender to bite (about 4 more minutes). Drain well; set vegetables and noodles aside separately.

Heat oil in same pan over medium-high heat. Add onion, basil, thyme, and oregano. Cook, stirring often, until onion is soft (about 7 minutes). Add turkey and cook, stirring occasionally, until no longer pink (about 5 minutes). Stir in marinara sauce; remove from heat.

Mix spinach and ricotta cheese; set aside.

Spread a third of the sauce in a shallow 2½- to 3-quart baking dish. Arrange half the noodles over sauce. Top noodles evenly with half *each* of the carrots, zucchini, spinach mixture, and mozzarella cheese. Repeat layers; then spread with remaining sauce. Sprinkle with Parmesan cheese.

Set baking dish in a shallow 10- by 15-inch baking pan to catch any drips. Bake lasagne, uncovered, in a 400° oven until hot in center (about 25 minutes). Let stand for 5 minutes before serving. Makes 6 servings.

Per serving: 627 calories, 35 g protein, 60 g carbohydrates, 30 g fat, 12 g saturated fat, 86 mg cholesterol, 1,403 mg sodium

SPEEDY CHILI WITH CORNMEAL DUMPLINGS

Preparation time: About 10 minutes

Cooking time: About 50 minutes

Cumin-seasoned cornmeal dumplings flecked with shredded cheese steam atop the chili they complement. For a change of pace, substitute red kidney beans or black beans for the cannellini.

2 **tablespoons salad oil**
1 **large onion, chopped**
1 **clove garlic, minced or pressed**
1 **pound ground turkey**
3 **tablespoons chili powder**
1 **large can (28 oz.) tomatoes**
2 **cans (about 15 oz. *each*) cannellini (white kidney beans), drained**
1 **can (4 oz.) diced green chiles**
   Dumpling Dough (recipe follows)

Heat oil in a 4- to 5-quart pan over medium-high heat. Add onion and garlic and cook, stirring often, until onion is soft (about 7 minutes). Add turkey and cook, stirring often, until no longer pink (about 5 minutes). Add chili powder, tomatoes (break up with a spoon) and their liquid, cannellini, and chiles. Bring to a boil; reduce heat to medium-low and simmer, uncovered, for 15 minutes.

Meanwhile, prepare Dumpling Dough.

After chili has simmered for 15 minutes, drop dough onto chili in about 2-tablespoon portions. Cover and simmer until dumplings are dry in center; cut to test (about 20 minutes). Makes 4 to 6 servings.

DUMPLING DOUGH. In a bowl, combine 1 cup **all-purpose flour,** ¼ cup **yellow cornmeal,** 1½ teaspoons **baking powder,** and ½ teaspoon *each* **ground cumin, dry sage leaves,** and **dry thyme leaves.** In another bowl, beat together 1 large **egg,** ½ cup **milk,** 1 tablespoon **salad oil,** and ½ cup shredded **Cheddar cheese.** Add egg mixture to flour mixture; stir just until moistened.

Per serving: 593 calories, 36 g protein, 62 g carbohydrates, 23 g fat, 6 g saturated fat, 124 mg cholesterol, 1,290 mg sodium

■ *Pictured on facing page*

TURKEY BURGERS WITH TOMATO SALAD

Preparation time: About 15 minutes

Cooking time: About 15 minutes

Enjoy this warm-weather meal for two outdoors on the patio. The dill-seasoned yogurt sauce is doubly refreshing—use half of it to dress the cucumber-tomato salad, the rest to top the moist burgers.

   Yogurt Sauce (recipe follows)
1 **medium-size red onion**
1 **teaspoon salad oil**
8 **ounces ground turkey**
½ **teaspoon ground cumin**
   Freshly ground pepper
¼ **cup water**
2 **tablespoons white wine vinegar or sherry vinegar**
2 **whole wheat pocket breads (*each* about 6 inches in diameter)**
1 **small cucumber (about 6 oz.), peeled and thinly sliced**
2 **small tomatoes, sliced**

Prepare Yogurt Sauce and refrigerate. Cut onion in half horizontally. Chop one half; thinly slice remaining half, separate into rings, and set aside.

In a 12- to 14-inch nonstick frying pan, combine chopped onion and oil. Cook over medium-high heat, stirring often, until onion is soft (about 7 minutes). Transfer to a bowl. Let cool slightly, mix with turkey and cumin, and season to taste with pepper. Shape mixture into 2 patties.

Place patties in pan and cook over medium-high heat, turning once, until browned on both sides (about 8 minutes). Pour off fat. Add water and vinegar. Reduce heat, cover, and simmer until almost all liquid has evaporated and patties are no longer pink in center; cut to test (about 7 more minutes).

Meanwhile, wrap pocket breads in foil and place in a 250° oven until hot (about 15 minutes). Also mix cucumber, onion rings, tomatoes, and half the Yogurt Sauce in a salad bowl.

Offer turkey patties with pocket breads, tomato salad, and remaining Yogurt Sauce. Makes 2 servings.

YOGURT SAUCE. In a small bowl, stir together 1 cup **plain nonfat yogurt,** ¼ cup **white wine vinegar** or sherry vinegar, and 2 tablespoons **dry dill weed.**

Per serving: 498 calories, 35 g protein, 57 g carbohydrates, 15 g fat, 4 g saturated fat, 59 mg cholesterol, 539 mg sodium

Ready for a different take on the familiar meat on a bun? Try Turkey Burgers with Tomato Salad (recipe on facing page). Heated pocket breads hold seasoned meat patties and a simple combination of cucumber, red onion, and tomatoes in a dill-seasoned yogurt sauce. Corn on the cob, fresh fruit, and lemonade complete a casual supper for two.

QUAIL & SQUAB SAMPLER

Pamper your dinner guests with some individual attention: serve them rich-tasting, all-dark-meat quail or squab. Just one squab is enough for a serving, but you'll usually want to allow two quail per person.

Sautéed quail in a buttery-smooth balsamic vinegar sauce make an impressive main course for your next small gathering. Grilled quail are just right for a patio party; try them with *pappardelle* (wide fettuccine) in fresh tomato-mushroom sauce.

Squab is especially tempting when soaked in a spicy marinade before roasting, then topped with tart lemon sauce. Or serve the birds skewered and grilled, acccompanied with a garlicky sweet-hot sauce.

QUAIL WITH ROSEMARY & BALSAMIC VINEGAR SAUCE

Preparation time: About 5 minutes

Cooking time: About 50 minutes

8 quail (about 4 oz. *each*), thawed if frozen
¼ cup butter or margarine
¾ cup regular-strength beef broth
½ cup balsamic vinegar
1 tablespoon chopped fresh rosemary leaves or 1 teaspoon dry rosemary

Reserve quail necks and giblets for other uses. Rinse quail inside and out; pat dry.

Melt 2 tablespoons of the butter in a 10- to 12-inch frying pan over medium-high heat. Add quail, about 4 at a time; do not crowd pan. Cook, turning as needed, until deep golden brown on all sides (about 20 minutes). Breast meat should be cooked through but still pink near bone; cut parallel to wing joint to test. Transfer quail to a serving dish and keep warm.

To pan, add broth, vinegar, and rosemary. Boil over high heat until reduced to ½ cup (about 5 minutes). Add remaining 2 tablespoons butter; reduce heat to medium and stir until butter is smoothly blended into sauce. Pour sauce over quail. Makes 4 servings.

Per serving: 499 calories, 40 g protein, 1 g carbohydrates, 36 g fat, 14 g saturated fat, 380 mg sodium*

■ *Pictured on page 7*

GRILLED QUAIL WITH PASTA

Preparation time: About 20 minutes

Cooking time: About 35 minutes

2 ounces sliced pancetta or bacon, diced
6 tablespoons olive oil
1 medium-size onion, thinly sliced
8 ounces mushrooms, quartered
2 cloves garlic, minced or pressed
6 medium-size pear-shaped tomatoes (about 12 oz. *total*), chopped
¼ cup slivered fresh sage leaves or 2 teaspoons dry sage leaves
1 cup dry white wine
8 quail (about 4 oz. *each*), thawed if frozen
Coarsely ground pepper
1 package (8½ oz.) dry pappardelle, 10 to 12 ounces fresh pappardelle, or 8 ounces dry extra-wide egg noodles
Salt
Sage sprigs and lemon wedges

Cook pancetta in a wide frying pan over medium heat until crisp. Remove from pan with a slotted spoon; drain and set aside. To pan drippings, add ¼ cup of the oil, then onion and mushrooms. Increase heat to medium-high and cook, stirring often, until mushrooms are lightly browned (about 5 minutes). Stir in garlic, tomatoes, slivered sage, and wine. Boil gently, uncovered, stirring occasionally, until sauce is slightly thickened (about 10 minutes).

Reserve quail necks and giblets for other uses. Then, with poultry shears or a knife, split quail lengthwise along one side of backbone. Pull quail open; place, skin side up, on a flat surface and press firmly, cracking bones slightly, until birds lie reasonably flat. Rinse quail and pat dry. Brush well with remaining 2 tablespoons oil; sprinkle with pepper.

Place quail, skin side down, on a lightly greased grill 4 to 6 inches above a solid bed of hot coals. Cook, turning as needed, until breast meat is cooked through but still pink near bone; cut parallel to wing joint to test (about 8 minutes). Lift from grill; keep warm.

Cook pasta according to package directions just until barely tender to bite. Drain well. Add pancetta to tomato sauce; season to taste with salt. Add pasta and mix lightly, using 2 spoons. Transfer to a large platter. Surround pasta with quail. Garnish with sage sprigs and lemon wedges. Makes 4 servings.

Per serving: 918 calories, 52 g protein, 52 g carbohydrates, 56 g fat, 13 g saturated fat, 230 mg sodium*

SQUAB WITH LEMON SAUCE

Preparation time: 15 minutes, plus 1 hour to marinate

Roasting time: About 20 minutes

  4 **squab (12 to 16 oz. *each*), thawed if frozen**
  ¼ **cup *each* soy sauce and dry sherry**
  2 **tablespoons Oriental sesame oil**
  2 **teaspoons honey**
  1 **teaspoon Chinese five-spice; or ¼ teaspoon *each* crushed anise seeds and ground cinnamon, cloves, and ginger**
     Lemon Sauce (recipe follows)

Reserve squab necks and giblets for other uses. With poultry shears or a knife, split squab lengthwise along one side of backbone. Pull squab open; place, skin side up, on a flat surface and press firmly, cracking bones slightly, until birds lie reasonably flat. Rinse squab, pat dry, and place in a large heavy-duty plastic bag.

In a bowl, mix soy, sherry, oil, honey, and five-spice; pour over squab. Seal bag; turn over several times to coat birds with marinade. Place bag in a large, shallow baking pan or dish; refrigerate for at least 1 hour or up to 1 day, turning bag over occasionally.

Drain squab; reserve marinade. Place squab, skin side up, on a rack in a 12- by 15-inch roasting pan. Roast, uncovered, in a 500° oven, brushing several times with marinade, until breast meat is cooked through but still pink near bone; cut parallel to wing joint to test (about 20 minutes). Meanwhile, prepare Lemon Sauce. Top squab with Lemon Sauce. Makes 4 servings.

Per serving without sauce: 968 calories, 58 g protein, 3 g carbohydrates, 78 g fat, 27 g saturated fat, 515 mg sodium*

LEMON SAUCE. Cut 2 large thin-skinned **lemons** into halves. Thinly slice one half; discard end pieces and any seeds. Set slices aside. Squeeze juice from remaining 3 lemon halves; you will need ¼ cup.

Heat 1 teaspoon **salad oil** in an 8- to 10-inch frying pan over high heat. Add 4 quarter-size slices **fresh ginger;** stir for 30 seconds. Add lemon slices, 1 cup **regular-strength chicken broth,** 3 tablespoons **sugar,** and the ¼ cup **lemon juice.** Bring to a boil; then reduce heat and simmer, uncovered, for 2 minutes.

Mix 1 tablespoon **cornstarch** with 2 tablespoons **water.** Pour into sauce and cook, stirring, until sauce boils and thickens. Add ½ to 1 teaspoon **soy sauce.** Discard ginger slices. Use sauce hot. Makes 1¼ cups.

Per tablespoon: 14 calories, 0 g protein, 3 g carbohydrates, 0 g fat, 0 g saturated fat, 0 mg cholesterol, 62 mg sodium

SQUAB, THAI STYLE

Preparation time: About 1 hour

Grilling time: About 20 minutes

     Thai Sauce (recipe follows)
  8 **squab (12 to 16 oz. *each*), thawed if frozen**
  ½ **cup minced fresh cilantro (coriander)**
  ⅓ **cup coarsely ground pepper**
  24 **cloves garlic, minced or pressed**

Prepare Thai Sauce and refrigerate. Reserve squab necks and giblets for other uses. With poultry shears or a knife, split squab lengthwise through breastbone. Pull squab open; place, skin side up, on a flat surface and press firmly, cracking bones slightly, until birds lie reasonably flat. Rinse; pat dry.

Thread squab on sturdy 18-inch metal skewers as follows. Force one skewer into drumstick and through thigh, then under backbone, through other thigh, and out other drumstick. Run a second skewer parallel to the first, forcing it through one side of breast and middle section of one wing, then over backbone, through middle section of other wing, and out other side of breast. Each pair of 18-inch skewers holds 2 or 3 squab.

Mash together cilantro, pepper, and garlic; rub evenly over squab. Place squab on a lightly greased grill 4 to 6 inches above a solid bed of medium coals. Cook, turning as needed, until breast meat is cooked through but still pink near bone; cut parallel to wing joint to test (about 20 minutes). Serve with Thai Sauce. Makes 8 servings.

Per serving without sauce: 948 calories, 59 g protein, 6 g carbohydrates, 75 g fat, 27 g saturated fat, 4 mg sodium*

THAI SAUCE. In a blender or food processor, combine 1 can (8 oz.) **tomato sauce,** 3 tablespoons firmly packed **brown sugar,** 6 cloves **garlic,** ⅛ to ½ teaspoon **ground red pepper** (cayenne), and ¼ cup **cider vinegar.** Whirl until blended. Add 1¼ cups **golden raisins** and ⅓ cup **water;** whirl to chop raisins coarsely. Pour sauce into a 2- to 3-quart pan; boil over high heat, stirring, until reduced to 1½ cups. Let cool, then cover and refrigerate until cold. Makes about 1½ cups.

Per tablespoon: 34 calories, 0 g protein, 9 g carbohydrates, 0 g fat, 0 g saturated fat, 0 mg cholesterol, 59 mg sodium

*Cholesterol data not available.

Serve Turkey Parmesan with Spaghetti (recipe on facing page) once, and you're bound to get requests for an encore! Cheese-topped ground turkey patties, a simple tomato sauce, and pasta add up to a guaranteed family favorite.

SPICY SAUSAGE

Preparation time: About 10 minutes

Cooking time: About 5 minutes

Some people think that breakfast just isn't breakfast without a few sizzling sausage patties. Unfortunately, the usual pork sausage doesn't fit the low-fat diets many of us are trying to establish. You can still start the day with the flavors you like, though: just make your own fragrant sausage from turkey breast, pepper, and fresh sage and rosemary.

1 **pound ground skinned turkey breast**

1 **teaspoon chopped fresh rosemary**

2 **teaspoons chopped fresh sage**

½ **teaspoon freshly ground pepper**

In a large bowl, combine turkey, rosemary, sage, and pepper. Form mixture into 8 patties, each 3 inches in diameter and about ¼ inch thick. Place patties in a 12- to 14-inch frying pan (preferably nonstick) and cook over high heat for 1 minute; then turn patties over and continue to cook for 1 more minute. Reduce heat. Continue to cook, turning occasionally, until patties are golden brown on outside and no longer pink in center; cut to test (about 3 more minutes). Makes 4 servings.

Per serving: 130 calories, 27 g protein, 0 g carbohydrates, 2 g fat, 1 g saturated fat, 70 mg cholesterol, 76 mg sodium

■ *Pictured on facing page*

TURKEY PARMESAN WITH SPAGHETTI

Preparation time: About 15 minutes

Cooking time: About 50 minutes

Spaghetti and meatballs? Veal Parmesan? This family favorite has elements of both. Herb-rich turkey patties boasting a double cheese coating of mozzarella and Parmesan are served on a bed of spaghetti with a tempting tomato-onion sauce.

Tomato-Onion Sauce (recipe follows)

1 **large egg**

½ **cup soft bread crumbs**

1⅓ **cups (about 7 oz.) grated Parmesan cheese**

½ **teaspoon poultry seasoning**

1 **pound ground turkey**

1 **tablespoon butter or margarine**

1 **tablespoon olive oil**

4 **slices mozzarella cheese (3 oz. *total*)**

8 **ounces dry spaghetti**

Italian parsley sprigs (optional)

Prepare Tomato-Onion Sauce; keep warm over lowest heat.

In a medium-size bowl, beat egg until blended. Add crumbs, ⅓ cup of the Parmesan cheese, and poultry seasoning; stir until blended. Add turkey; mix lightly until well combined. Shape turkey mixture into 4 patties, each about 4 inches in diameter.

Melt butter in oil in a 12- to 14-inch frying pan over medium-high heat. Add turkey patties and cook, turning once, until browned on both sides (about 8 minutes). Transfer patties to a shallow baking or broiling pan. Spread each patty with 2 tablespoons of the Tomato-Onion Sauce; then top each with 1 slice of the mozzarella cheese and 1 tablespoon of the remaining Parmesan cheese.

Just before broiling patties, cook spaghetti according to package directions just until tender to bite. Drain well, transfer to a deep platter, and keep warm.

Broil turkey patties about 4 inches below heat until cheeses are melted and lightly browned (about 3 minutes).

To serve, spoon remaining Tomato-Onion Sauce over spaghetti, then top with turkey patties. Garnish with parsley, if desired. Offer remaining ¾ cup Parmesan cheese to add to taste. Makes 4 servings.

TOMATO-ONION SAUCE. Heat 2 tablespoons **olive oil** or salad oil in a 2-quart pan over medium heat. Add 1 medium-size **onion,** finely chopped; 2 teaspoons **dry oregano leaves;** 1 **dry bay leaf;** and 1 large clove **garlic,** minced or pressed. Cook, stirring often, until onion is soft but not browned (about 10 minutes). Stir in 1 large can (15 oz.) **tomato sauce.** Bring to a boil; then reduce heat, cover, and simmer for 20 minutes, stirring occasionally.

Per serving: 764 calories, 46 g protein, 57 g carbohydrates, 39 g fat, 14 g saturated fat, 154 mg cholesterol, 1,323 mg sodium

CHUNKY TURKEY SAUCE WITH PENNE

Preparation time: About 15 minutes

Cooking time: About 1¾ hours

When the weather is cold and you'd rather cozy up to a fire than venture outdoors, try this hearty pasta meal. Once you've started the sauce, you can settle down with a favorite book and keep an eye on the simmering pot. (Don't skimp on the cooking time; the flavor improves as the sauce boils down.)

- 2 tablespoons olive oil
- 1 large onion, finely chopped
- 1 clove garlic, minced or pressed
- 1 medium-size green bell pepper, seeded and finely chopped
- 2 medium-size carrots, finely shredded
- 8 ounces mushrooms, thinly sliced
- 2 tablespoons chopped parsley
- 2 teaspoons dry basil leaves
- 1 teaspoon dry rosemary
- 1 pound ground turkey
- 2 large cans (28 oz. *each*) pear-shaped tomatoes
- 1 large can (12 oz.) tomato paste
- ½ cup dry red wine
- 1 dry bay leaf
- 1 pound dry penne

Heat oil in a 4- to 5-quart pan over medium-high heat. Add onion, garlic, bell pepper, carrots, mushrooms, parsley, basil, and rosemary. Cook, stirring often, until vegetables are soft (about 15 minutes). Remove vegetables from pan, transfer to a bowl, and set aside.

Add turkey to pan; cook over medium-high heat, stirring often, until no longer pink (about 5 minutes). Return vegetables to pan; add tomatoes (break up with a spoon) and their liquid, tomato paste, wine, and bay leaf. Increase heat to high and bring mixture to a boil; then reduce heat to medium-low, cover, and boil gently, stirring often, for 30 minutes. Uncover and continue to cook, stirring occasionally, until sauce is reduced to 8 cups (about 45 more minutes). Remove and discard bay leaf.

Cook penne according to package directions just until tender to bite. Drain well. Place in a large, shallow serving bowl, top with sauce, and mix lightly. Makes 8 servings.

Per serving: 424 calories, 22 g protein, 65 g carbohydrates, 10 g fat, 2 g saturated fat, 41 mg cholesterol, 726 mg sodium

SPAGHETTI SQUASH WITH CREAMY TURKEY

Preparation time: About 10 minutes

Cooking time: About 1¼ hours

If your dinner guests haven't encountered spaghetti squash before, they'll marvel at the magical way it separates into long, pastalike strands. The mild vegetable "spaghetti" is the perfect partner for a delicate, nutmeg-scented meat sauce.

- 1 spaghetti squash (2 to 3 lbs.)
- 2 tablespoons olive oil
- ¼ cup finely chopped shallots
- 1 pound ground turkey
- ¼ cup butter or margarine
- 1 cup whipping cream
- ½ cup dry white wine
- 1 cup (about 5 oz.) grated Parmesan cheese
- ½ teaspoon ground nutmeg

Pierce spaghetti squash in several places with a fork; then place in a shallow baking pan. Bake, uncovered, in a 350° oven until shell gives when pressed (about 1¼ hours; turn squash over after 45 minutes). Keep warm until ready to serve.

About 20 minutes before squash is done, heat oil in a 10- to 12-inch frying pan over medium-high heat. Add shallots and cook, stirring often, for 1 minute. Add turkey and cook, stirring often, until no longer pink (about 5 minutes). Add butter, cream, and wine; stir to melt butter. Reduce heat to medium-low and simmer, uncovered, stirring occasionally, until thickened (about 10 minutes). Stir in cheese and nutmeg.

Cut baked squash in half; scrape out and discard seeds. Loosen squash strands with a fork, then scoop strands out onto a rimmed platter. Spoon sauce over squash. Makes 6 servings.

Per serving: 503 calories, 25 g protein, 13 g carbohydrates, 38 g fat, 19 g saturated fat, 139 mg cholesterol, 627 mg sodium

MINCED TURKEY IN LETTUCE

Preparation time: About 15 minutes, plus 30 minutes to soak mushrooms

Cooking time: About 8 minutes

Nestled in crisp lettuce cups, this speedy stir-fry of turkey and vegetables is bursting with flavor. The meal is just as good with ground chicken or with thin strips of turkey or chicken breast.

    Cooking Sauce (recipe follows)
  3 medium-size dried shiitake mushrooms
    (*each* about 2 inches in diameter)
  1 tablespoon salad oil
  2 cloves garlic, minced or pressed
1½ teaspoons grated fresh ginger
  ½ teaspoon crushed dried hot red chiles
  1 pound ground skinned turkey breast
  1 can (about 8 oz.) sliced bamboo shoots,
    drained and minced
  1 can (about 8 oz.) water chestnuts, drained
    and minced
  6 green onions (including tops), minced
  ½ cup frozen peas, thawed
 12 large lettuce leaves
    Hoisin sauce (optional)

Prepare Cooking Sauce and set aside. Soak mushrooms in warm water to cover for 30 minutes, then drain. Cut off and discard stems; squeeze caps dry, thinly slice, and set aside.

Heat oil in a 10- to 12-inch frying pan over medium-high heat. Add garlic, ginger, and chiles; stir once. Then add turkey and cook, stirring often, until no longer pink (about 5 minutes). Remove turkey mixture from pan and set aside.

Add bamboo shoots, water chestnuts, onions, and mushrooms to pan; cook, stirring, for 2 minutes. Return turkey mixture to pan along with peas. Then stir in Cooking Sauce and cook, stirring, until sauce is thickened.

To serve, coat center of a lettuce leaf with hoisin, if desired. Spoon some of the turkey mixture on top, then roll up and eat out of hand. Makes 6 servings.

COOKING SAUCE. In a small bowl, stir together 2 teaspoons **cornstarch**, 1 tablespoon **dry sherry**, 2 tablespoons *each* **reduced-sodium soy sauce** and **water,** and ½ teaspoon **sugar.**

Per serving: 163 calories, 20 g protein, 12 g carbohydrates, 4 g fat, 1 g saturated fat, 47 mg cholesterol, 272 mg sodium

SORREL-SCENTED BROTH WITH TURKEY

Preparation time: About 25 minutes

Cooking time: About 10 minutes

Hot broth and the lemony accent of sorrel seem perfectly suited to crisp autumn days. Celebrate the season with this soup—there's sorrel in both the simple broth and the tender meatballs.

  ¾ cup lightly packed sorrel leaves, washed,
    stems removed
  2 or 3 slices white bread, crusts removed
  1 pound ground turkey
  1 large egg
  8 cups regular-strength chicken broth
  ⅛ teaspoon white pepper
    About ½ teaspoon salt (or to taste)
  4 strips lemon peel (colored part only), *each*
    ½ by 4 inches
  2 medium-size carrots, cut into julienne
    strips
  2 to 3 tablespoons lemon juice

Finely chop half the sorrel leaves. Cut remaining leaves into thin shreds. Set sorrel aside.

Tear bread into small pieces and whirl in a blender or food processor to make ¾ cup fine crumbs. In a large bowl, mix crumbs, chopped sorrel, turkey, egg, ¼ cup of the broth, pepper, and salt.

In a 5- to 6-quart pan, combine lemon peel and remaining 7¾ cups broth. Bring to a boil over high heat. Drop turkey mixture into boiling broth in tablespoon-size portions, then add carrots. Reduce heat, cover, and simmer until turkey meatballs are no longer pink in center; cut to test (about 5 minutes). Skim and discard fat from broth; remove and discard lemon peel, if desired. Add lemon juice.

Ladle meatballs and soup into 6 wide soup bowls; sprinkle sorrel shreds over each serving. Makes 6 servings.

Per serving: 215 calories, 20 g protein, 10 g carbohydrates, 11 g fat, 2 g saturated fat, 74 mg cholesterol, 1,615 mg sodium

Convenient Cooked Poultry

DICED & CHUNKED & CHILLED & TOSSED &

DRESSED & SOUPED & SHREDDED & MINCED &

WRAPPED & SLAWED & SANDWICHED & STACKED &

*The family will urge you to roast a turkey just so they can enjoy
the leftovers in Turkey Pot Pie (recipe on page 124). Peppery cream cheese
pastry covers a savory blend of cooked poultry, yams, kale, and leeks.
You won't need elaborate accompaniments—try a green salad or perhaps
a dish of sweet peas tossed with enoki mushrooms.*

CHICKEN & LEMON GRASS SOUP

Preparation time: About 15 minutes

Cooking time: About 35 minutes

Lemon grass adds its citrusy flavor and fragrance to many Thai and Vietnamese dishes. The bulbous-based stalks, quite similar in appearance to green onions, are sold in most Asian grocery stores and in many larger supermarkets. Here, lemon grass combines with some distinctly non-Asian ingredients—among them jalapeños and avocado—in an appetizing first-course soup.

  1 **stalk fresh lemon grass**

  1 **large can (49½ oz.) regular-strength chicken broth**

 ⅛ **teaspoon freshly ground pepper**

  1 **fresh jalapeño chile, seeded and minced**

  1 **clove garlic, minced or pressed**

 ½ **cup thinly sliced green onions (including tops)**

 ½ **cup chopped fresh cilantro (coriander)**

  1 **medium-size firm-ripe tomato, seeded and coarsely chopped**

  2 **cups bite-size pieces cooked chicken or turkey**

  1 **medium-size firm-ripe avocado**

Trim and discard root end and leaves from lemon grass; peel off and discard coarse outer layers of stalk. In a 4- to 5-quart pan, combine lemon grass, broth, pepper, chile, and garlic. Bring to a boil over high heat; then reduce heat, cover, and simmer for 30 minutes. Discard lemon grass. Stir in onions, cilantro, tomato, and chicken; heat through.

    Pit, peel, and chop avocado. Evenly divide avocado among 6 soup bowls; then ladle soup over avocado. Makes 6 servings.

Per serving: 179 calories, 18 g protein, 5 g carbohydrates, 10 g fat, 2 g saturated fat, 42 mg cholesterol, 1,063 mg sodium

HOT CHICKEN & SAVOY SALAD

Preparation time: About 25 minutes

Frilly ornamental kale, also known as salad savoy, adds color to this main-course salad. The sweet leaves hold their texture and tint when heated briefly; tossed with shredded chicken and sliced oranges, they make the perfect meal for a dark, chilly day.

 12 **ounces salad savoy**

  2 **large oranges (about 1 lb. *total*)**

  2 **tablespoons white wine vinegar**

  1 **teaspoon minced fresh rosemary; or 1 teaspoon dry rosemary, crumbled**

  1 **clove garlic, minced or pressed**

 ¼ **to ½ teaspoon crushed dried hot red chiles**

 ⅓ **cup salad oil**

 ¼ **cup thinly sliced green onions (including tops)**

1½ **cups shredded cooked chicken**

    Salt and pepper

Remove and discard tough stems from salad savoy; wash and drain leaves, then tear into bite-size pieces (you should have about 8 cups). Set aside.

    Grate enough peel from one orange to make 1 teaspoon. In a small dish, mix grated orange peel, vinegar, rosemary, garlic, and chiles; set aside. Then, using a sharp knife, cut peel and all white membrane from both oranges. Thinly slice oranges crosswise; cut each slice in half.

    Heat oil in a 12- to 14-inch frying pan or 5- to 6-quart pan over medium-high heat. Add onions and cook, stirring, until limp (about 2 minutes). Add vinegar mixture and salad savoy; cook, stirring, just until leaves begin to wilt slightly (about 1 minute).

    Remove savoy mixture from heat; turn into a large bowl, arrange oranges and chicken on top, and toss to mix. Season to taste with salt and pepper. Makes 4 servings.

Per serving: 341 calories, 19 g protein, 19 g carbohydrates, 22 g fat, 3 g saturated fat, 47 mg cholesterol, 85 mg sodium

CHICKEN-GRAPEFRUIT SALAD ON AVOCADOS

Preparation time: About 15 minutes

Presented on buttery avocado halves and topped with juicy pink grapefruit, this refreshing salad will keep the cook out of the kitchen and the company at the table. Fresh tarragon and a pinch of cayenne pepper enliven the creamy dressing that coats celery, green onions, and chunks of chicken.

Tarragon-Pepper Dressing (recipe follows)

2 cups bite-size pieces cooked chicken breast

½ cup thinly sliced celery

¼ cup thinly sliced green onions (including tops)

3 large firm-ripe avocados

1 tablespoon lemon juice

2 large pink grapefruits

6 medium-size red leaf lettuce leaves, washed and crisped

Prepare Tarragon-Pepper Dressing; add chicken, celery, and onions and mix to coat with dressing. Set aside.

Halve, pit, and peel avocados; coat with lemon juice. Using a sharp knife, cut peel and all white membrane from grapefruits; then cut segments free and set them aside.

Place a lettuce leaf on each of 6 salad plates; set an avocado half, pitted side up, on lettuce on each plate. Spoon a sixth of the chicken salad over each avocado half, then top salads equally with grapefruit segments. Makes 6 servings.

TARRAGON-PEPPER DRESSING. In a large bowl, mix ⅓ cup *each* **mayonnaise** and **sour cream,** 2 teaspoons **white wine vinegar,** 1 tablespoon chopped **fresh tarragon leaves** or 1 teaspoon dry tarragon leaves, 1 teaspoon minced **parsley,** ⅛ teaspoon **ground red pepper** (cayenne), and ¼ teaspoon **black pepper.**

Per serving: 430 calories, 19 g protein, 19 g carbohydrates, 33 g fat, 7 g saturated fat, 53 mg cholesterol, 133 mg sodium

CHERIMOYA CHICKEN SALAD

Preparation time: About 10 minutes

Don't let its reptilian appearance scare you away! Beneath the cherimoya's leathery, almost scaly-looking skin is fragrant flesh with a custardy texture and a pineapple-banana flavor. Cut into wedges, the sweet fruit complements chicken chunks and thin cucumber slices in a tart lemon dressing.

¼ cup olive oil or salad oil

¼ cup lemon juice

1½ teaspoons *each* grated lemon peel and sugar

½ teaspoon pepper

1½ cups bite-size pieces cooked chicken breast

1 piece (about 7 inches long) European-style cucumber (about 8 oz.), quartered lengthwise, then thinly sliced

3 green onions (including tops), thinly sliced

8 medium-size butter lettuce leaves, washed and crisped

1 ripe cherimoya (about 12 oz.), quartered lengthwise

Lemon wedges

Salt

In a large bowl, stir together oil, lemon juice, lemon peel, sugar, and pepper; spoon out 2 tablespoons of this dressing and reserve. Add chicken to remaining dressing in bowl, then stir in cucumber and onions.

Arrange 2 lettuce leaves on each of 4 dinner plates; top leaves with equal amounts of salad. Set a cherimoya wedge on each plate; drizzle fruit evenly with the reserved 2 tablespoons dressing, then garnish with lemon wedges. Season to taste with salt. Makes 4 servings.

Per serving: 282 calories, 18 g protein, 19 g carbohydrates, 16 g fat, 2 g saturated fat, 45 mg cholesterol, 45 mg sodium

*This is definitely not the same old salad! Creative but surprisingly
simple, Lemon Chicken Salad in Radicchio (recipe on facing page) combines
pine nuts, fresh lemon wedges, chicken, and radicchio with a touch of oil. Serve
with iced tea, warm herb bread, and your favorite marinated beans.*

LEMON CHICKEN SALAD IN RADICCHIO

Preparation time: About 20 minutes, plus at least 1 hour to crisp radicchio

Brighten up the buffet with a colorful chicken salad served in purple-red radicchio leaves. Because the salad is so simple, it's important to use a flavorful, good-quality olive oil, such as a fruity extra-virgin variety.

- 2 **heads radicchio (about 1 lb. *total*), *each* 3 to 4 inches in diameter**
- ¼ **cup pine nuts**
- 1 **large lemon, thinly sliced**
- 2 **cups minced cooked chicken breast**
- 2 **tablespoons extra-virgin olive oil**
  Salt and pepper

Remove 8 large radicchio leaves; rinse leaves and radicchio heads. Wrap in paper towels, enclose in a plastic bag, and refrigerate until crisp (at least 1 hour) or for up to 2 days.

Spread pine nuts in an 8- or 9-inch-diameter baking pan. Toast, uncovered, in a 350° oven until lightly browned (about 8 minutes), shaking pan occasionally. Set aside.

Discard seeds from lemon slices. Cut 2 slices into quarters and set aside. Cut each remaining slice into 10 wedges. In a large bowl, mix small lemon wedges with pine nuts, chicken, and oil. (At this point, you may cover and refrigerate until next day.)

Finely shred radicchio heads; discard cores. Mix shredded radicchio with chicken mixture, then season to taste with salt and pepper.

Set reserved radicchio leaves on a large platter; mound chicken salad equally in leaves. Garnish with reserved lemon quarter-slices. Makes 6 to 8 servings.

Per serving: 143 calories, 15 g protein, 5 g carbohydrates, 8 g fat, 1 g saturated fat, 34 mg cholesterol, 37 mg sodium

OLIVE-PECAN CHICKEN SLAW

Preparation time: About 15 minutes

Cole slaw? How ordinary! Well, not always. This main-dish slaw does feature the requisite shredded cabbage and slightly sweetened dressing, but it also holds apple chunks, ripe olives, chicken, and crisp butter-toasted pecans. Line the salad bowl with whole cabbage leaves for an attractive presentation.

- 2 **teaspoons butter or margarine**
- ½ **cup pecan halves**
  Lemon-Mustard Dressing (recipe follows)
- 2 **cups shredded green cabbage**
- 1½ **cups bite-size pieces cooked chicken breast**
- 1 **medium-size Red Delicious apple, cored and diced**
- 1 **jar (2 oz.) diced pimentos, drained**
- 1 **can (2¼ oz.) sliced ripe olives, drained**
- ¼ **cup thinly sliced celery**
  Salt

Melt butter in a 8- to 10-inch frying pan over medium-low heat. Add pecans and cook, stirring occasionally, until nuts smell toasted and look golden inside; break a nut to test (about 7 minutes). Set aside on paper towels to drain.

Prepare Lemon-Mustard Dressing. Then add cabbage, chicken, apple, pimentos, olives, and celery to dressing; stir to blend. Sprinkle pecans over salad; season to taste with salt. Makes 4 servings.

LEMON-MUSTARD DRESSING. In a salad bowl, stir together ½ cup **mayonnaise**, 2 tablespoons **lemon juice**, 1 teaspoon **Dijon mustard** or regular prepared mustard, ½ teaspoon **sugar**, and ¼ teaspoon **pepper**.

Per serving: 455 calories, 19 g protein, 15 g carbohydrates, 37 g fat, 6 g saturated fat, 67 mg cholesterol, 410 mg sodium

Feature

GLORIOUS GOOSE & PHEASANT

Dinner is always a celebration if you serve goose or pheasant: when these birds come to the table, it's a safe bet that the cook has put some careful planning— and often a lot of time—into the meal. Happily, our recipes reward both cooks and diners for that extra effort.

If you're after a truly magnificent feast, offer a rich roast goose, stuffed with herbed cabbage. Roast pheasant is impressive, too; try it with a creamy white wine and chanterelle sauce. For a special meal for two, offer sautéed pheasant breasts with lime-pistachio butter and cranberry sauce.

Both goose and pheasant are usually sold frozen, but you can buy them fresh in some supermarkets during the holiday season or order them almost all year round from specialty meat markets or game farms.

GOLDEN GOOSE WITH CABBAGE-APPLE STUFFING

Preparation time: About 1 hour

Roasting time: 2 to 3 hours

- 1 **goose (8 to 12 lbs.), thawed if frozen**
- 2 **medium-size lemons**
- 1 **tablespoon olive oil or salad oil**
- 1½ **pounds green cabbage, cored and finely shredded**
- 4 **cups coarsely chopped peeled Golden Delicious apples**
- 1 **cup golden raisins**
- ¾ **cup chopped parsley**
- ½ **teaspoon *each* dry marjoram leaves, dry thyme leaves, dry chervil leaves, dry sage leaves, and ground allspice**
- ½ **cup unsweetened white grape juice or apple juice**
  Pepper
  Parsley sprigs and lemon wedges

Reserve goose neck and giblets for other uses. Pull off and discard lumps of fat from goose. Rinse goose inside and out; pat dry. With a fork, prick

skin all over goose at about 1½-inch intervals. Cut one of the lemons in half. Rub and gently squeeze one half all over inside of goose; set remaining lemon half and whole lemon aside.

Heat oil in a 5- to 6-quart pan over medium-high heat. Add cabbage and apples; cover and cook, stirring occasionally, until cabbage is wilted (about 8 minutes). Remove from heat and stir in raisins, chopped parsley, marjoram, thyme, chervil, sage, and allspice. Grate peel from remaining whole lemon and stir into cabbage mixture. Then squeeze juice from this lemon and stir into grape juice; set aside.

Stuff body and neck cavities of goose with cabbage mixture; skewer cavities closed. Rub outside of goose with remaining lemon half; sprinkle goose all over with pepper. Place goose, breast down, on a V-shaped rack in a 12- by 17-inch roasting pan. Cover goose with a tent of foil, sealing foil to pan edges.

Roast goose in a 350° oven for 1 hour. Uncover; siphon off and discard fat from pan. Turn goose breast up and insert a meat thermometer in thickest part of a drumstick (not touching bone). Continue to roast, uncovered, siphoning off fat and basting bird with grape juice mixture every 30 minutes, until thermometer registers 175°F (1 to 2 more hours).

Transfer goose to a large platter. Remove skewers, then spoon stuffing out onto platter next to bird. Garnish with parsley sprigs and lemon wedges. Makes 6 to 8 servings.

Per serving: 1,101 calories, 80 g protein, 34 g carbohydrates, 71 g fat, 22 g saturated fat, 283 mg cholesterol, 239 mg sodium

PHEASANTS & CHANTERELLES

Preparation time: About 20 minutes

Cooking time: About 1 hour

- 2 pheasants (about 2½ lbs. *each*), thawed if frozen
- 2 tablespoons salad oil
- 1 cup *each* coarsely chopped onion, carrots, and celery
- 10 dry juniper berries
- 6 whole cloves
- 1 clove garlic, minced or pressed
- 1 teaspoon minced fresh sage leaves or ¼ teaspoon dry sage leaves

  About 3 cups water
- 4 slices bacon

  Mushroom Sauce (recipe follows)

  Salt and white pepper

Remove and rinse pheasant necks; reserve giblets for other uses. Rinse birds inside and out; pat dry.

Heat oil in a 12- to 14-inch frying pan over medium-high heat. Add whole birds and necks; cook, turning as needed, until browned on all sides (about 10 minutes). Place birds, breast up, on a rack in a 12- by 15-inch roasting pan; set aside.

Leave necks in frying pan; then add onion, carrots, celery, juniper berries, cloves, garlic, and sage to pan. Cook over medium heat, stirring often, until onion is soft. Add 3 cups of the water. Bring to a boil over high heat; then boil until liquid is reduced by half (about 10 minutes). Pour mixture through a fine strainer; discard vegetables and necks. Measure strained stock; you need 1 cup. If necessary, boil to reduce to 1 cup or add water to increase amount. Skim and discard fat from stock; set stock aside for Mushroom Sauce.

Drape pheasants with bacon. Roast, uncovered, in a 400° oven, basting often with pan juices, until breast meat is white with a touch of pink near bone (about 30 minutes). To test, cut to breastbone parallel to wing joint; meat should look moist, not soft and wet.

While pheasants are roasting, prepare Mushroom Sauce. When pheasants are done, pour any pan juices into Mushroom Sauce; heat sauce through and season to taste with salt and pepper. Remove bacon from pheasants. With poultry shears or a heavy knife, cut each pheasant in half lengthwise along backbone and through breastbone. Place pheasant halves on a platter; top with Mushroom Sauce. Makes 4 servings.

MUSHROOM SAUCE. In frying pan used to brown pheasants, melt 2 tablespoons **butter** or margarine over medium-high heat. Add ¾ teaspoon minced **garlic,** 1 tablespoon minced **shallot,** and 3 cups (9 oz.) **chanterelles** or thinly sliced button mushrooms.

Cook, stirring often, until mushrooms are lightly browned and all liquid has evaporated (about 5 minutes). Stir 2 tablespoons **all-purpose flour** into mushroom mixture; smoothly stir in **reserved vegetable-pheasant stock** and 1 cup **dry white wine.** Boil, uncovered, stirring often, until reduced by a third (about 5 minutes). Add ½ cup **whipping cream** and bring to a boil. Remove from heat.

Per serving: 1,259 calories, 116 g protein, 12 g carbohydrates, 81 g fat, 28 g saturated fat, 444 mg sodium*

PHEASANT BREASTS WITH PISTACHIO BUTTER

Preparation time: About 20 minutes

Cooking time: About 6 minutes

- Pistachio Butter (recipe follows)
- 2 pheasant breast halves (about 6 oz. *each*), breastbone removed (may have wing joint attached)
- ½ teaspoon coarsely ground pepper
- 2 tablespoons butter or margarine
- ¾ cup fresh or frozen cranberries
- 1 tablespoon sugar
- Parsley sprigs (optional)

Prepare Pistachio Butter; set aside.

Rinse pheasant and pat dry. If wing joints are attached, cut them off and set aside. Pull off and discard all skin and fat from breast halves. Place each breast half between 2 sheets of plastic wrap; pound with a flat-surfaced mallet to a thickness of ⅛ to ¼ inch. Sprinkle meat with pepper.

Melt butter in a 10- to 12-inch frying pan over medium-high heat. When butter sizzles, add pounded breast halves and wing sections. Cook, turning as needed, until breasts are lightly browned on both sides but still slightly pink in center; cut to test (about 4 minutes). Place a breast half on each dinner plate. Top each serving with Pistachio Butter; keep warm.

To pan with wing sections, add cranberries and sugar. Reduce heat to low and cook, stirring often, until berries just begin to pop (about 1 minute). Spoon cranberries equally onto breast pieces beside Pistachio Butter. Add a wing section to each plate; garnish with parsley, if desired. Makes 2 servings.

PISTACHIO BUTTER. Mince ¼ cup **salted roasted pistachio nuts.** Place in a small bowl and add 2 tablespoons **butter** or margarine (at room temperature), 1 tablespoon minced **parsley,** ¼ teaspoon grated **lime peel,** and 1 teaspoon **lime juice.** Mix well.

Per serving: 585 calories, 48 g protein, 16 g carbohydrates, 37 g fat, 17 g saturated fat, 297 mg sodium*

*Cholesterol data not available.

CHINESE HOT & SOUR CHICKEN NOODLE SALAD

Preparation time: About 10 minutes

Cooking time: About 15 minutes

Here's a tempting cold pasta salad that fits right into a healthful diet. Chile-flavored oil mixed with soy and a generous splash of mellow rice vinegar dresses linguine, cool cucumber slices, and shredded chicken breast.

- 8 **ounces dry linguine**
- 3 **tablespoons salad oil**
- ¾ **teaspoon crushed dried hot red chiles**
- 1 **tablespoon Sichuan peppercorns, toasted and ground (see page 51); or 1 tablespoon whole black peppercorns, ground**
- ⅓ **cup rice vinegar or cider vinegar**
- 2 **tablespoons reduced-sodium soy sauce**
- ¼ **cup chopped fresh cilantro (coriander)**
- 1 **small cucumber, thinly sliced**
- 1½ **cups shredded cooked chicken breast**

Cook linguine according to package directions just until tender to bite. Drain; immerse in cold water until cool, then drain well again. Set aside.

Heat oil in a 6- to 8-inch frying pan over low heat. Add chiles; cook just until chiles begin to brown (about 3 minutes). Let cool, then add ground peppercorns, vinegar, soy, and cilantro.

In a shallow dish, arrange a bed of linguine; cover with cucumber and chicken. Pour dressing evenly over salad and mix to blend. Makes 4 servings.

Per serving: 407 calories, 25 g protein, 47 g carbohydrates, 13 g fat, 2 g saturated fat, 45 mg cholesterol, 345 mg sodium

■ *Pictured on facing page*

BARBECUE CHICKEN PIZZA PIE

Preparation time: About 50 minutes

Baking time: About 25 minutes

Are you ready for pizza pie, Southern style? Skip the traditional tomato sauce and mozzarella cheese; instead, top the crust with homemade barbecue sauce, chicken, jack cheese, and bell pepper. Serve with a simple salad for down-home satisfaction.

- **Barbecue Sauce (recipe follows)**
- 1 **package (10 oz.) refrigerated pizza dough; or 1 package (1 lb.) frozen white bread dough, thawed**
- 2 **cups diced or shredded cooked chicken**
- 1 **large red bell pepper, seeded and thinly sliced**
- 2 **cups (8 oz.) shredded plain or chile-seasoned jack cheese**
- **Cilantro (coriander) sprigs**

Prepare Barbecue Sauce; set aside.

Press dough over bottom and up sides of a lightly greased 14-inch-diameter pizza pan or shallow 10- by 15-inch baking pan. Pierce dough with a fork at 2-inch intervals. Bake on bottom rack of a 400° oven until light golden (about 10 minutes).

In a bowl, mix chicken and Barbecue Sauce. Spread mixture evenly over baked crust. Arrange bell pepper over chicken mixture, then sprinkle evenly with cheese. Return to oven and bake on bottom rack until cheese is bubbly (about 15 minutes). Garnish with cilantro. Cut into wedges or rectangles to serve. Makes 6 servings.

BARBECUE SAUCE. Melt 2 tablespoons **butter** or margarine in a 10- to 12-inch frying pan over medium heat. Add 1 large **onion,** thinly sliced; cook, stirring occasionally, until onion is golden brown (about 25 minutes). Add ½ cup *each* **catsup** and **tomato-based chili sauce,** ¼ cup **cider vinegar,** and 1 tablespoon *each* **molasses** and **Worcestershire.** Bring to a boil over high heat; then reduce heat and simmer, uncovered, for 10 minutes. If made ahead, let cool; then cover and refrigerate for up to 2 days.

Per serving: 457 calories, 28 g protein, 39 g carbohydrates, 20 g fat, 3 g saturated fat, 85 mg cholesterol, 1,079 mg sodium

If you like barbecued chicken and pizza, why not enjoy both in one dish?
Barbecue Chicken Pizza Pie (recipe on facing page) may not be traditional, but
that doesn't lessen its appeal. Sweetened with molasses and spiced with chiles,
the pie is complemented by chunky potato salad and dill-seasoned okra.

CHICKEN-BROCCOLI QUICHE WITH ALMONDS

Preparation time: About 30 minutes

Baking time: About 45 minutes

Take advantage of the chicken you saved from yesterday's dinner to create a new meal tonight. An easy pat-in pastry crust holds a rich, nutmeg-scented custard filled with chicken, broccoli, and Gruyère—so good that no one will even think "leftovers"!

- **Pat-in Crust (recipe follows)**
- 8 ounces broccoli
- 3 large eggs
- 1 cup half-and-half or milk
- ¼ teaspoon *each* ground nutmeg and pepper
- 1 cup finely chopped cooked chicken
- 1 cup (4 oz.) shredded Gruyère or Swiss cheese
- 2 tablespoons sliced almonds

Prepare Pat-in Crust; set aside. Reduce oven temperature to 350°.

Trim and discard tough ends of broccoli stalks; then peel and thinly slice remainder of stalks. Cut flowerets into about ¾-inch pieces. Then arrange all broccoli on a rack in a 2- to 3-quart pan above 1 inch of boiling water. Cover and steam until broccoli is tender when pierced (about 5 minutes). Let cool.

In a bowl, beat eggs, half-and-half, nutmeg, and pepper until blended. In another bowl, mix broccoli, chicken, and cheese; spread evenly in crust. Pour egg mixture over chicken mixture; sprinkle with almonds. Bake in a 350° oven until center appears set when pan is gently shaken (about 45 minutes). Let stand for at least 15 minutes before cutting into wedges. Makes 6 servings.

PAT-IN CRUST. In a 9-inch pie pan, combine 1½ cups **all-purpose flour** and ½ cup (¼ lb.) **butter** or margarine, cut into chunks. Rub together with your fingers until mixture resembles fine crumbs. Add 1 large **egg;** stir until dough clings together. Then press dough evenly over bottom, sides, and rim of pie pan. Bake on bottom rack of a 375° oven until pale golden (about 10 minutes).

Per serving: 496 calories, 23 g protein, 29 g carbohydrates, 33 g fat, 18 g saturated fat, 239 mg cholesterol, 309 mg sodium

CHICKEN ENCHILADA BAKE

Preparation time: About 20 minutes

Baking time: About 30 minutes

How can such a hearty and richly flavored casserole be perfect fare for the diet-conscious diner? Simple—the tortillas are baked (not fried), the meat is skinless chicken breast, and the sauce is made with low-sodium broth and low-fat yogurt. Top with Cheddar cheese for an extra taste treat.

- 12 corn tortillas (*each* 6 to 7 inches in diameter)
- 5 medium-size tomatoes, peeled and thinly sliced
- 2 cups shredded cooked chicken breast
- 1 cup thinly sliced green onions (including tops)
- 1 tablespoon butter or margarine
- 2 tablespoons all-purpose flour
- 2 cups low-sodium chicken broth
- 1 cup plain low-fat yogurt
- 1 can (4 oz.) diced green chiles
- ½ cup finely shredded Cheddar cheese

Dip tortillas, one at a time, in water; let drain briefly. Stack tortillas; cut stack into 8 wedges. Then spread a third of the tortilla wedges in a 9- by 13-inch baking pan. Top with half the tomatoes; cover with half *each* of the chicken and onions. Repeat layers, ending with tortillas. Set aside.

Melt butter in a 2- to 3-quart pan over medium heat. Add flour and cook, stirring, until bubbly. Whisk in broth and bring to a boil. Remove from heat, add yogurt and chiles, and whisk until smooth. Pour over tortillas in baking pan.

Cover and bake in a 375° oven for 20 minutes. Uncover, sprinkle with cheese, and continue to bake, uncovered, until cheese is melted (about 10 more minutes). Makes 8 servings.

Per serving: 254 calories, 19 g protein, 28 g carbohydrates, 8 g fat, 3 g saturated fat, 43 mg cholesterol, 291 mg sodium

CHICKEN CARBONARA

Preparation time: About 10 minutes

Cooking time: About 20 minutes

Adding pine nuts and diced chicken to classic pasta *carbonara* creates a delightful new tradition. Serve with lightly dressed salad greens and crisp whole wheat bread sticks.

- ½ **cup pine nuts**
- 4 **slices bacon, chopped**
- 8 **ounces dry linguine or 1 package (9 oz.) fresh linguine**
- 4 **large eggs**
- ½ **cup grated Parmesan cheese**
- ⅓ **cup whipping cream**
- ¼ **cup chopped parsley**
- ¼ **cup chopped fresh basil leaves or 2 tablespoons dry basil leaves**
- 3 **cloves garlic, minced or pressed**
- 1½ **cups diced cooked chicken**
- 1 **to 2 tablespoons butter or margarine**

Toast pine nuts in a 10- to 12-inch frying pan over medium-low heat until lightly browned (about 3 minutes), shaking pan often. Remove from pan and set aside in a large bowl. Increase heat to medium; add bacon to pan and cook, stirring often, until browned (about 7 minutes). Lift out bacon with a slotted spoon; place in bowl with nuts. Reserve drippings in pan.

Cook linguine according to package directions just until tender to bite. Drain well.

While pasta is cooking, add eggs, cheese, cream, parsley, basil, garlic, and chicken to bacon and pine nuts. Beat until well mixed.

To reserved bacon drippings in frying pan, add enough butter to make ¼ cup; melt butter in drippings over medium-low heat. Add linguine, then egg mixture. Mix lightly, using 2 forks, until linguine is well coated with egg mixture. Makes 4 servings.

Per serving: 755 calories, 40 g protein, 49 g carbohydrates, 46 g fat, 17 g saturated fat, 316 mg cholesterol, 508 mg sodium

MINI TURKEY TAMALES

Preparation time: About 1¼ hours

Cooking time: About 45 minutes

Substituting squares of foil for the standard corn husk wrappers cuts down on the time it takes to prepare tamales. Filled with a robust mixture of salsa, olives, and turkey, these savory little bundles can be served as a main course or an appetizer.

- 2 **cups dehydrated masa flour (corn tortilla flour)**
- 1¼ **cups regular-strength chicken broth**
  Salt
- ½ **cup salad oil**
- 2 **cups finely diced cooked turkey or chicken**
- ½ **cup pitted ripe olives, coarsely chopped**
- 1 **medium-size onion, finely chopped**
- ½ **cup prepared green chile salsa**

Cut thirty 6-inch-square pieces of foil. In a large bowl, combine masa flour, broth, ½ teaspoon salt, and oil; stir together to make a thick paste. Spread about 1½ tablespoons of the paste in a 3-inch square in center of each piece of foil.

In a bowl, mix turkey, olives, onion, and salsa; season to taste with salt. Spoon about 1½ tablespoons of the filling down center of each masa-dough square. Fold foil edges together so masa edges meet; then seal all sides.

Stack wrapped tamales, arranging loosely so steam can circulate, in a large pan on a rack above at least 1 inch of boiling water. Cover; adjust heat to keep water at a steady boil. Cook, adding boiling water as needed to maintain water level, until masa dough is firm to touch; unwrap a tamale to test (about 45 minutes). Makes 30 small tamales, 6 main dish servings.

Per serving: 406 calories, 18 g protein, 32 g carbohydrates, 23 g fat, 3 g saturated fat, 36 mg cholesterol, 643 mg sodium

Yesterday's turkey gets dressed up for today's dinner with the help of juicy orange slices and an easy sour cream sauce. Served over fresh cheese- or meat-filled spinach pasta, Turkey with Tortellini & Oranges (recipe on facing page) is worthy of your most important company.

TURKEY WITH TORTELLINI & ORANGES

Preparation time: About 25 minutes

Cooking time: About 20 minutes

Pick out a pretty serving platter—this main dish really deserves to be shown off! Orange slices surround fresh tortellini and turkey chunks topped with a chive-sprinkled sour cream sauce.

- 3 **large oranges (about 1½ lbs.** *total)*
- 7 **cups regular-strength chicken broth**
- 1½ **pounds fresh cheese- or meat-filled plain or spinach tortellini**
- 3 **cups diced or shredded cooked turkey**
- 2 **teaspoons celery seeds**
- 2 **cups sour cream**
- ¼ **cup snipped chives**

Using a vegetable peeler, cut a 6-inch-long, 1-inch-wide strip of peel (colored part only) from one of the oranges. Cut strip into long, thin shreds and set aside. Then, using a sharp knife, cut peel and all white membrane from all 3 oranges. Cut each orange crosswise into 6 slices; set slices aside.

In a 5- to 6-quart pan, bring broth to a boil over high heat. Add tortellini and cook just until tender to bite (about 4 minutes; or time according to package directions). With a slotted spoon, lift out tortellini and transfer to a platter; keep warm.

To broth in pan, add turkey, celery seeds, and shredded orange peel; cook just until turkey is heated through. Lift out turkey with a slotted spoon and arrange atop tortellini. Place sour cream in a small pan, then stir in 3 tablespoons of the chives and ½ cup of the hot broth (reserve remaining broth for other uses). Stir broth–sour cream mixture over low heat just until hot, then spoon over turkey. Sprinkle with remaining 1 tablespoon chives; arrange orange slices around turkey and pasta. Makes 6 servings.

Per serving: 694 calories, 46 g protein, 68 g carbohydrates, 27 g fat, 11 g saturated fat, 150 mg cholesterol, 1,752 mg sodium

TURKEY QUICHE

Preparation time: About 35 minutes

Baking time: About 30 minutes

Leftovers are cause for culinary celebration when you transform yesterday's roast turkey and stuffing into filling and crust for today's quiche. Layered with cheese, onions, and mushrooms, this creamy, custardy pie is a satisfying and thrifty supper.

- 5 **large eggs**
- 2½ **to 3 cups leftover bread stuffing; or half of a 6-ounce package bread stuffing mix, prepared according to package directions**
- 1 **cup (4 oz.) shredded Gruyère or Swiss cheese**
- 1 **cup diced cooked turkey or chicken**
- ¼ **cup thinly sliced green onions (including tops)**
- ½ **cup sliced mushrooms**
- 1 **cup half-and-half**
  Salt and pepper

In a bowl, beat one egg until blended; then add stuffing and mix well. Press stuffing mixture over bottom and up sides of a greased 10-inch pie pan or deep quiche pan or dish. Bake, uncovered, on lowest rack of a 425° oven until stuffing is crisp and dry to the touch (about 15 minutes). Remove from oven; reduce oven temperature to 350°.

Sprinkle cheese over bottom and sides of stuffing crust, then top crust evenly with turkey, onions, and mushrooms.

In bowl used to prepare stuffing crust, beat remaining 4 eggs to blend; then stir in half-and-half and season to taste with salt and pepper. Pour over turkey and vegetables. Bake on lowest rack of oven until filling appears set when pan is gently shaken (about 30 minutes). Let stand for at least 10 minutes before cutting into wedges. Makes 6 servings.

Per serving: 464 calories, 23 g protein, 26 g carbohydrates, 30 g fat, 15 g saturated fat, 272 mg cholesterol, 725 mg sodium

■ *Pictured on page 111*

TURKEY POT PIE

Preparation time: About 30 minutes

Cooking time: About 30 minutes

The rich cream cheese pastry crust for this pie bakes separately while the turkey-vegetable filling cooks on your stove.

    Parmesan-Pepper Pastry (recipe follows)
1 **tablespoon butter or margarine**
½ **cup thinly sliced leeks (white part only)**
2½ **cups regular-strength chicken broth**
½ **cup Madeira or regular-strength chicken broth**
1 **pound yams or sweet potatoes, peeled and cut into ½-inch cubes**
½ **teaspoon** *each* **dry sage leaves and dry thyme leaves**
3 **tablespoons cornstarch mixed with 3 tablespoons water**
8 **ounces kale, washed, stems removed, and leaves chopped**
3 **cups bite-size pieces cooked turkey**

Prepare Parmesan-Pepper Pastry.

While pastry is baking, melt butter in a 5- to 6-quart pan over medium heat. Add leeks; cook, stirring, until soft (about 3 minutes). Add broth, Madeira, yams, sage, and thyme. Bring to a boil; reduce heat, cover, and simmer until yams are tender when pierced (about 20 minutes). Stir cornstarch mixture into broth. Add kale and turkey; bring to a boil, stirring.

Pour turkey mixture into casserole used to shape pie crust. Loosen hot pastry from foil on baking sheet; then slide it onto turkey mixture. To serve, break through pastry with a spoon, dipping out filling with pastry. Makes 6 servings.

PARMESAN-PEPPER PASTRY. In a food processor, combine 1 cup **all-purpose flour,** ½ cup grated **Parmesan cheese,** ½ teaspoon **pepper,** and 1 large package (8 oz.) **cream cheese,** cut into large chunks. Whirl until dough forms a ball.

On a 12- by 15-inch sheet of foil, invert a shallow 2- to 2½-quart casserole. With tip of a knife, lightly trace around edge of casserole. Set casserole aside.

In center of outline, pat pastry out ½ inch thick; lightly dust with **all-purpose flour.** Roll pastry out until it extends ¼ inch beyond outline. Fold edge of pastry under ¼ inch; crimp edge. With a sharp knife or cookie cutter, make one or more cutouts through pastry; take care not to tear foil. With a fork, pierce pastry at ½-inch intervals just inside edge (to keep pastry from puffing excessively as it bakes).

Slide pastry on foil onto a 12- by 15-inch baking sheet. Bake, uncovered, in a 350° oven until golden (about 30 minutes). Use hot.

Per serving: 502 calories, 31 g protein, 45 g carbohydrates, 21 g fat, 12 g saturated fat, 106 mg cholesterol, 697 mg sodium

CHINESE STIR-FRIED TURKEY

Preparation time: About 20 minutes

Marinating time: At least 30 minutes or up to 1 day

Cooking time: About 7 minutes

At the end of a tiring day, this zippy stir-fry wakes up the tastebuds without wearing out the cook.

    Spiced Marinade (recipe follows)
3 **cups shredded cooked turkey or chicken**
2 **tablespoons salad oil**
1½ **tablespoons minced fresh ginger**
2 **cloves garlic, thinly sliced**
3 **small dried hot red chiles**
2 **cups shredded napa cabbage**
3 **stalks celery, sliced diagonally**
1 **cup 1-inch pieces green onions (including tops)**
1½ **cups julienne strips jicama**

Prepare Spiced Marinade. Stir in turkey, cover, and refrigerate for at least 30 minutes or up to 1 day.

Heat oil in a wok or 12- to 14-inch frying pan over medium-high heat. Add ginger, garlic, and chiles; stir until garlic is golden (about 1½ minutes). Add cabbage, celery, onions, and jicama; cook, stirring, until celery is barely tender-crisp to bite (about 3 minutes). Add turkey mixture; stir until sauce comes to a full boil. Discard chiles, if desired. Makes 4 servings.

SPICED MARINADE. In a large bowl, stir together 1 cup **regular-strength chicken broth;** 2 tablespoons **cornstarch;** 2 tablespoons *each* **soy sauce** and **oyster sauce;** 2 tablespoons **dry sherry** or regular-strength chicken broth; 1 tablespoon **Oriental sesame oil;** and ½ teaspoon *each* **anise seeds** and **ground cinnamon.**

Per serving: 354 calories, 35 g protein, 17 g carbohydrates, 16 g fat, 3g saturated fat, 82 mg cholesterol, 1,232 mg sodium

INDEX

Good looks aren't everything, but they certainly make Game Hens
with Mustard Crust (recipe on page 36) even more appealing. A mustard
coating enriched with garlic and rosemary gives the butterflied birds a
flavor every bit as wonderful as their tempting appearance.

127